Scorecards for Results

Scorecards for Results

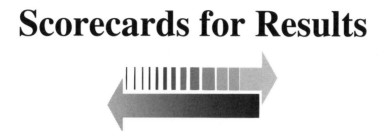

A Guide for Developing a Library Balanced Scorecard

Joseph R. Matthews

A Member of the Greenwood Publishing Group

Westport, Connecticut • London

Library of Congress Cataloging-in-Publication Data

Matthews, Joseph R.
  Scorecards for results : a guide for developing a library balanced scorecard /
  Joseph R. Matthews.
    p. cm.
  Includes bibliographical references and index.
  ISBN 978-1-59158-698-2 (alk. paper)
  1. Public libraries—Evaluation. I. Title.
Z678.85.M39 2008
027.4—dc22
2008003689

British Library Cataloguing in Publication Data is available.

Library of Congress Catalog Card Number: 2008003689
ISBN: 978-1-59158-698-2

First published in 2008

Libraries Unlimited, 88 Post Road West, Westport, CT 06881
A Member of the Greenwood Publishing Group, Inc.
www.lu.com

Printed in the United States of America

∞™

The paper used in this book complies with the
Permanent Paper Standard issued by the National
Information Standards Organization (Z39.48–1984).

10 9 8 7 6 5 4 3 2 1

This workbook was developed as a part of an Institute of Museum and Library
Services 2004-05 National Leadership Grant LG-02-04-0050-04. Any views,
findings, conclusions or recommendations expressed in this workbook do not
necessarily represent those of the Institute of Museum and Library Services.

Contents

Acknowledgments

This workbook was developed as part of an Institute of Museum and Library Services 2004–2005 National Leadership Grant (LG-02-04-0050-04). Any views, findings, conclusions, or recommendations expressed in this workbook do not necessarily represent those of the Institute of Museum and Library Services.

It is important to acknowledge the initial four public libraries whose balanced scorecard journeys made this workbook possible: the Carlsbad City Library, the Cerritos Library, the Chula Vista Public Library, and the Newport Beach Public library, all located in southern California. The project is particularly indebted to the public libraries which agreed to put the workbook through a test drive during 2005–2006.

This workbook was prepared based on the literature and the experiences of ALL these libraries and provides a process that will assist any library in developing its own balanced scorecard.

The preparation of this book was also enhanced by the timely and responsive interlibrary loan service provided by Teri Roudenbush and her staff at the California State University, San Marcos, library. Thanks also to the wonderful folks at Libraries Unlimited, especially Ron Maas and Sue Easun. As usual, the text of this book has benefited from the wonderful and skillful editing of Sharon DeJohn.

Foreword

A library is a marvelous resource, a source of knowledge and experience that can influence a community for generations into the future. But how does one know what that public good really is and if those who are the custodians are actually achieving it? The answer to this question is the same for libraries as it is for any organization: (1) Clearly define your mission and (2) show through measurement that the mission is being executed. This is easily said, but application in practice is far more complex.

The balanced scorecard (BSC) was developed to help organizations deal with this complexity. The BSC is, in part, a methodology for developing a suite of measures that describe the organization's strategy. More important, the BSC is a philosophy of management: Put strategy at the center of the way in which you manage your library. By using the language of measurement to describe your strategy and to guide your day-to-day actions, your chances of successfully executing your mission are dramatically enhanced.

The balanced scorecard has been in use for over a decade. It has been applied successfully in organizations from around the world in virtually every industry and public sector niche. In this important work, Joe Matthews provides a roadmap to bring the benefits of the balanced scorecard to libraries and librarians. As the title implies, the book is a practical guide to the design and use of a BSC program. It is based on best practice experiences in libraries, as well as other organizations. This roadmap has worked for others and will work for you if you have the diligence to pursue it.

I commend the author for the clarity of his message and highly recommend the work. In particular, I encourage you to apply the balanced scorecard approach to your organization. The BSC is not a "silver bullet" that will magically produce results overnight. Instead, it is a commitment to a journey—a journey to your vision of the future guided by your new BSC navigation system. I wish you the best on that journey. We citizens have much to gain from your success.

David P. Norton
Boston, Massachusetts

Introduction

A planning process will assist any library in developing a strategic plan that ultimately answers the questions: Who are our customers, and how shall we serve them? A good planning process will help a library select a few service responses that will meet a community's identified needs. Note that a community might be a city or county, the students and faculty of an academic institution, or employees of a government agency or company.

Rather than attempting to be all things to all customers, a tendency that too many libraries have fallen victim to over the years, the planning process will help a library focus its services in an effort to differentiate itself from its competitors. The result, it is hoped, will be that the library will do a better job for its customers.

The important question that is yet to be addressed is: What manageable set of statistics and performance measures will best present a complete picture of the performance and value of the library? It is the goal of this workbook to answer this question.

PERFORMANCE MEASURES

Many writers have observed that, "what gets measured gets done," an epigram that the performance measurement community uses to communicate the essential message that use of performance measures affects behavior.[1] Performance measurements are used to effect behavioral change within the library.

Robert Orr first expressed the view that it was possible to consider performance measures as a continuum reflecting the transformation of resources into goods or services and ultimately having an impact or effect on an individual and society, as shown in Figure I.1.

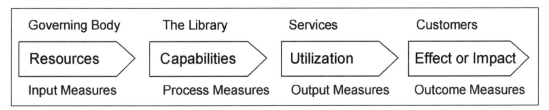

Figure I.1. General Evaluation Model. Adapted from R. H. Orr, "Progress in Documentation—Measuring the Goodness of Library Services: A General Framework for Considering Quantitative Measures," *Journal of Documentation* 29, no. 3 (September 1973), 315–32.

The *resources* provided to a library are transformed and organized so that the library has the *capability* to provide a set of services. The library customers then *utilize* these services, which should have a direct beneficial *impact* or *effect* on the individual and directly or indirectly upon the local community.

Input measures are associated with the resources, sometimes called inputs, that have been allocated to the library, such as money. The monetary budget is then converted into other inputs: staff, information technology infrastructure, facilities, and equipment. The library profession has a long history of using input measures, especially when comparing one library with other comparable libraries, when attempting to justify budget increases or when introducing a new service.

How efficiently the resources are transformed into the potential or capabilities to deliver services is reflected in *process measures*. Process measures usually quantify the time or cost involved in performing a specific task or activity. Process measures are particularly revealing when comparing the performance of one library with other comparable libraries. Efficient allocation of resources demonstrates that resources have not been wasted. Efficiency measures are designed to answer the question: Are we doing *things right*?

Output measures point to the degree to which the library and its services are being utilized. They are usually counts that measure volume of activity. Some libraries have long used output measures as an indication of success—the rationale of such an assumption being that the more the library's collection and services are used, the better.

> *Counting outputs is important, but must be kept in proportion. The world has changed. More is not necessarily better; it can just mean information overload.*
>
> —Jennifer Cram and Valerie Shine[2]

Outcome measures indicate the impact or effects of library services on a specific individual and ultimately on the library's community. As shown in Figure I.2, it is possible to further segment the likely outcomes of a library by focusing first on the individual and then on the community or organization.

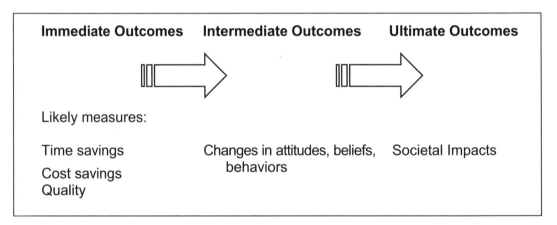

Figure I.2. Possible Outcome Subdivisions

Reliable library outcome measures are difficult to envision and formulate without the additional problem of attempting to gather the required data in a cost efficient manner. The use of various synonyms to characterize the "effects" of a library can help in this process:

- **Outcome**: the consequence, practical result, or effect of an event or activity

- **Impact:** the effect or influence of one person, thing, action, or service on another

- **Value:** the importance of something; the perception of actual or potential benefit

- **Benefit:** the helpful or useful effect that a thing or service has[3]

Palmer found evidence that organizations concentrate on measuring what is easily measurable, which results in a bias toward measuring performance in terms of economy and efficiency, rather than focusing on effectiveness.[4]

An extension of Orr's performance spectrum model answers the "How, Who, What, and Why" questions, as shown in Figure I.3.

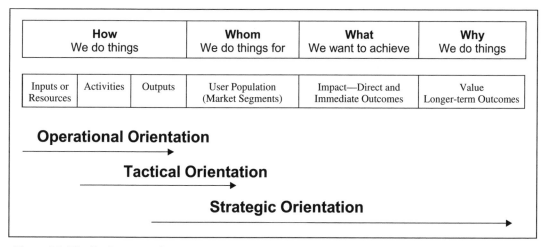

How We do things	**Whom** We do things for	**What** We want to achieve	**Why** We do things

Inputs or Resources	Activities	Outputs	User Population (Market Segments)	Impact—Direct and Immediate Outcomes	Value Longer-term Outcomes

Operational Orientation

Tactical Orientation

Strategic Orientation

Figure I.3. The Performance Spectrum. Adapted from Jennifer Cram and Valerie Shine, "Performance Measurement as Promotion: Demonstrating Benefit to Your Significant Others" (Paper presented at the School Library Association of Queensland Biennial Conference, June 29–July 1, 2004, Gold Coast, Queensland). Available at http://www.alia.org.au/~jcram/PMasPromotion.pdf.

A focus on *operations* is reflected in the use of input and process performance measures. A *tactical* orientation involves the use of process and output measures. A *strategic* orientation requires the use of output measures—to demonstrate use of the library (an implied value) as well as use of outcome measures.

WHY ADOPT THE USE OF A BALANCED SCORECARD

The challenge facing any organization, including a library, is when to seriously consider adopting a tool or technique that will bring real change to the organization. The answer to this question for most libraries is NOW! The fact is, if you keep doing what you've always done, you'll keep getting what you always have. A library scorecard is particularly valuable because it:

- **Helps the library to better understand what drives the demand for library services.** The scorecard is an organizational development tool that will assist in identifying the causes and effects of different strategies. It facilitates setting organizational objectives and providing feedback on strategy.

- **Helps the library demonstrate accountability.** In order to be accountable and demonstrate results, the library has to measure its true performance. Simple counts of activities no longer suffice.

- **Helps library staff be more responsive to customer needs.** The balanced scorecard will assist the library in focusing on its customers rather than on its internal operations. Too often the library examines itself from an inward-looking and backward-looking perspective.

- **Helps the library better communicate its value.** A balanced scorecard can assist the library in better communicating to its funding decision makers and other stakeholders by presenting a more "balanced" view of the library and its impact on its community. The use of the scorecard will also improve accountability of financial resources.

- **Helps library staff members focus on the importance of achieving the library's goals.** The balanced scorecard can be an effective tool for communicating the library's goals to employees so that each staff member better understands how his or her job contributes to meeting those goals.

- **Helps library management better understand performance measures.** A balanced scorecard will assist the library management team in selecting the most important performance measures as well as understanding the relationships between them.

- **Helps the library move beyond short-term problem solving.** The balanced scorecard is a tool that will assist all levels of staff members in better understanding the strategies the library has chosen to employ as it strives to reach its vision.

- **Encourages staff to move beyond opinions to a position of constructive problem analysis and resolution.** The use of performance measures provides concrete data on which to make sound decisions, thus reducing the urge to manage by intuition. Amos Lakos has called for the development of a "culture of assessment."[5]

- **Helps the library improve services.** Improvement is impossible without measurement. If you don't know where you are, then it is difficult to know where you are going, and you certainly can't get to where you want to be. It's analogous to attempting to cross rugged terrain without a compass, a map, or an ultimate destination.

As demonstrated throughout this book, the library balanced scorecard offers an important methodology that will enable a library to more effectively focus its resources, provide feedback about the actual impact of the library's strategies, better serve its community, and communicate the library's value to its stakeholders and its community in a beneficial manner.

HOW TO USE THIS WORKBOOK

The scorecard team members should first read chapters 1 through 3 of this workbook to gain an understanding of the balanced scorecard concept, the potential adjustments that can be made, and the steps necessary for creating the library's own library balanced scorecard. Thereafter, the scorecard team members should read a chapter or two prior to each meeting in order to be prepared to more effectively participate in the process itself.

Additional resources are suggested at the end of chapter 1 for those who wish to delve deeper into the concept of the balanced scorecard.

WHAT'S IN THIS WORKBOOK?

- Chapter 1 introduces the concept of the balanced scorecard.

- Chapter 2 discusses the importance of creating a library balanced scorecard that reflects the library's unique mission and vision.

- Chapter 3 provides an overview of the six-step process that should be followed by a library to develop its own scorecard.

- Chapter 4 discusses the importance of the library creating or revising its mission and vision statements.

- Chapter 5 reviews the alternative strategies that the library can choose and introduces the concept of a strategy map.

- Chapter 6 examines how the library can identify what performance measures are important and are linked to its strategies.

- Chapter 7 looks at the need for the library to choose short-term and long-term targets for performance measures. In addition, the library may need to identify various initiatives required to achieve its target goals.

- Chapter 8 argues the need for the library to integrate the balanced scorecard into its weekly and monthly meetings.

- Chapter 9 presents alternative ways the library can present its scorecard to its stakeholders.

- A glossary provides definitions for terms that may be unfamiliar to the reader.

- The Appendix contains some recommended readings about a number of topics related to developing a scorecard and using performance measures.

NOTES

1. Jennifer Cram and Valerie Shine, "Performance Measurement as Promotion: Demonstrating Benefit to Your Significant Others" (Paper presented at the School Library Association of Queensland Biennial Conference, June 29–July 1, 2004, Gold Coast, Queensland). Available at http://www.alia.org.au/~jcram/PMasPromotion.pdf.

2. Cram and Shine, "Performance Measurement as Promotion."

3. Roswitha Poll, "Measuring the Impact and Outcome of Libraries," *Performance Measurement and Metrics* 4, no. 1 (2003): 5–12.

4. Anna J. Palmer, "Performance Measurement in Local Government," *Public Money and Management* 13, no. 4 (October–December 1993): 31–36.

5. Amos Lakos. "Culture of Assessment as a Catalyst for Organizational Culture Change in Libraries." In *Proceedings of the Fourth Northumbria International Conference on Performance Measurement in Libraries and Information Service, 12 to 16 August 2001*, 311–20 (New Castle, UK: University of Northumbria, 2002).

1

What Is a Balanced Scorecard?

Governing boards of many different types of organizations, including libraries, complain that lack of time and crowded agendas result in spending little time discussing strategy and learning what really drives the demand for service.[1] Primarily for historical reasons, the vast majority of libraries collect a plethora of internally focused performance measures and statistical information. Some of these measures are reported to the library's stakeholders, some are used to complete annual surveys required by various organizations, and sadly, many are gathered but then ignored.

The goal of this workbook is to assist the library in determining what performance measures and metrics are important within a broader context of strategic planning and management. These important measures should focus on what defines the success of the library and shows the difference it makes in the lives of customers.

The balanced scorecard is not another "go out and measure everything" exercise. Keeping score by itself does not reveal anything about how to win the game. The scorecard helps keep track of the progress a library is making in achieving its goals. Using performance measures in and of themselves does nothing unless the measures inform management's actions.

The balanced scorecard responds well to a number of challenges and offers the hope of assisting a library through that murky minefield called strategic management.

ORIGINS OF THE BALANCED SCORECARD

In the 1990s Robert Kaplan, a Harvard accounting professor, and David Norton, a consultant, collaborated on a project to develop a set of performance measures that would complement the heavily weighted financial measures found in almost all company annual reports.[2] Financial measures by their very nature are backward-looking or lagging measures and reflect results of the prior month, previous quarter, or last year. The result of this project was development of the balanced scorecard.

The performance measures selected for the balanced scorecard should reflect the vision and strategies of the organization and include four viewpoints or perspectives: financial, customer, internal business processes, and learning and growth (sometimes called organizational readiness, innovation, and learning or potentials). Within each perspective, three to five measures are chosen to reflect the strategic goals and vision of the organization. The balanced scorecard is shown in graphic form in Figure 1.1 (page 2).

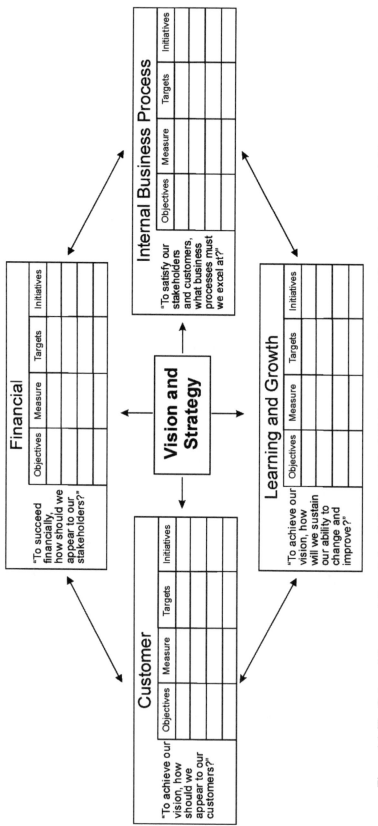

Figure 1.1. The Balanced Scorecard. From Robert S. Kaplan and David P. Norton, "Using the Balanced Scorecard as a Strategic Management System," *Harvard Business Review* (January–February 1996): 76. Reprinted with permission.

Originally developed to fit the needs of for-profit companies, the balanced scorecard has been successfully adapted by governments and nonprofit organizations, as discussed in greater detail in chapter 2.

The balanced scorecard, as shown in Figure 1.2 (page 4), is "read" from the bottom to the top. In essence, the scorecard requires the organization to create a cause-and-effect relationship between the perspectives. For example, if a company invests in additional training for its staff and provides the necessary information technology infrastructure (the organizational readiness, or learning and growth, perspective), then the staff members will be better able to develop improvements in procedures and processes (the internal processes, or internal business process, perspective) and thus work more productively. The staff will also be better able to respond to customer needs and requests, which will lead to more satisfied customers (the customer perspective), which in turn will lead to higher revenues and better profits (the financial perspective).

The four perspectives are designed to balance:

- The financial and nonfinancial

- The inward-facing (process) and outward-facing (customer satisfaction) measures

- Performance drivers (leading indicators) and outcome measures (lagging measures)

- Current performance and the future

Once the organization is able to clearly articulate its strategy, it will create a strategy map, which is a graphic method for showing how its strategy is reflected in each perspective. Performance measures are then chosen to reflect the selected strategies, and both short-term and long-term targets for each measure are identified. The data for each measure are collected as required (data may be collected by an automated system as the result of each transaction, or sampled periodically, ranging from short periods of time to annually). The balanced scorecard is typically updated and the results are presented on a quarterly basis.

Characteristics of organizations that have found the balanced scorecard a useful and effective tool include

- an organizational culture that is oriented toward improvement, measurement, and performance;

- management commitment to implementing and maintaining the use of the scorecard;

- training and educating staff so that they understand the value of the scorecard;

- clear, simple, and regular reporting of the results using the scorecard; and

- updating the scorecard on a monthly or quarterly basis.[3]

The Organizational Readiness Perspective

This perspective, sometimes called "learning and growth," "innovation and learning," or "potentials," is designed to assess the library's ability to compete in the future. The organization may assess the skills of its employees to determine whether the right mix and depth of skills are present to meet the changing competitive environment. The information technology readiness assessment is designed to ensure that the IT network and software applications meet the needs of the organization today and into the future. The organization may also wish to determine whether its organizational culture will support a climate for change and action, as reflected in employee morale and the staff turnover rate.

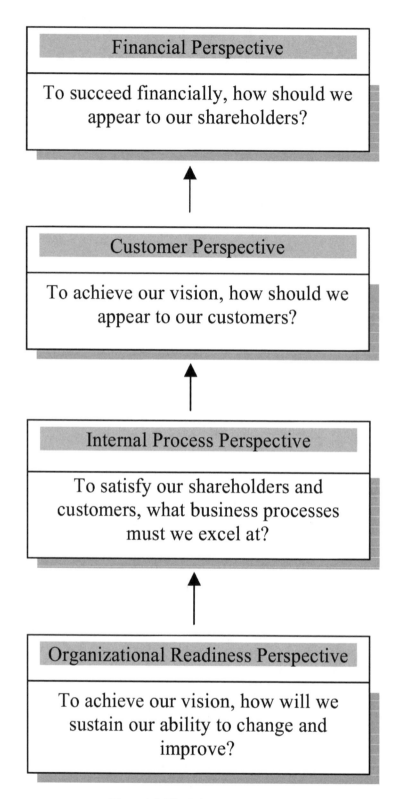

Figure 1.2. The Balanced Scorecard

This perspective attempts to answer the following type of questions:

- Are staff members equipped with the right skills to deliver quality services?
- Are new technologies being tracked so that skills likely to be needed in the future are being identified?
- Do staff members have the proper tools and training to perform their jobs in an excellent manner?
- Is the library's IT infrastructure (local area network, link to the Internet, and application software) adequate to meet the needs of the library today and into the near-term future?
- Are the morale and motivation of library staff members high?
- Does the library have a culture that is willing to carefully and systematically assess the quality of services currently being delivered?
- Does the library have the appropriate number of branches? Are its physical facilities of sufficient size and well maintained?

The Internal Process Perspective

The goal of the internal process perspective is to understand the processes and activities critical to enabling the library to satisfy its customer needs and that add value in the eyes of customers. In developing its balanced scorecard, the library should be identifying and implementing the strategies that will allow it to offer distinctive and sustainable competitive advantages.

Usually costs, quality, throughput, productivity, and time issues are included in this perspective. Quality improvement initiatives attempt to monitor and improve existing library practices and processes by eliminating non-value-added work and streamlining workflows. In developing its own scorecard, the library may identify new services, and hence processes, in which it must excel in order to meet customer expectations and the changing conditions of the marketplace.

There are many methodologies and techniques available to support improvement (whether continuous/incremental or radical) of internal processes and procedures. These include process reengineering, advocated by Michael Hammer and James Champy;[4] activity modeling; data modeling; activity based costing (ABC); cost-benefit analysis; total quality management; and Six Sigma, among others.

The challenges that arise when a library focuses on its processes include

- involving staff in the measurement of their work and processes;
- analyzing process data using statistical control techniques;[5]
- focusing in the wrong areas (measuring processes that have the greatest impact on customers); and
- failing to understand the big picture (changes made to improve one process may negatively affect the operation of a broader group of activities).

The Customer Perspective

For any organization, the heart of its business strategy is the customer value proposition that allows the organization to differentiate itself from it competitors. The performance measures or indicators chosen for this perspective show the extent to which the company is serving its potential market (market share) and how well the customers' needs are met by the products or services being delivered (customer satisfaction measures).

Customers generally evaluate a product or service by considering three discrete categories of benefits: product or service attributes, relationship, and image or brand name.

Possible *product or service attributes* of interest to a customer are:

- **Availability.** Does the organization have the product or service when it is requested by the customer? For a library, this translates into whether the desired item is on the shelf or the service can be delivered. An availability study or fill rate survey is often used to determine how often the library is able to provide the desired item.

- **Selection.** Some organizations compete by providing a wide variety of products or services (for example, Nordstrom's in the retail sector), whereas others offer fewer choices and compete using other service attributes.

- **Quality.** Many organizations compete in the marketplace on the basis of high quality (for example, Mercedes or Lexus in the automobile sector). It is important to note, however, that a great many organizations have been spending considerable time and energy on quality improvement projects, so that high quality is now often an assumption made by customers.

- **Functionality.** Some organizations find that providing a greater amount of product functionality, for example, a software application, will differentiate them from their competitors. The challenge for those that wish to compete is that the bar is constantly being raised, and what is superior functionality today will become the minimum standard in a year or two.

- **Time.** Assuming the customer makes a decision to physically visit the library, the time and energy required to retrieve the desired material or receive a service may be considerable. The customer may also need to wait in a queue for assistance or to receive a service. Ultimately the customer makes a determination about whether the effort involved exceeds the likely value of the information or materials being sought.

  The determination of customer value versus effort in an information setting such as a library has been formalized as "Mooers' Law," which states: "An information retrieval system will tend not to be used whenever it is more painful and troublesome for a customer to have information than for him not to have it."[6]

- **Price.** The customer incurs a cost to fulfill an information need, even if the materials or information service is "free," as in most libraries. Given the low price of using the tax-supported public library, an important question to ponder is why more citizens are not using the library. Clearly the answer involves a number of factors; however, competition is obviously one of the more important concerns.

The *relationship* that exists between the customer and an organization can be manifest in two ways:

- **Service.** The service provided to its customers may be one of the most important differentiating factors in the customer value proposition. For example, some of the higher priced four- and five-star hotels maintain an extensive customer profile so that customer preferences are anticipated and provided without any action on the part of the guest. The goal is to develop a level of customer intimacy such that the customer would never consider staying at a hotel with a different name on the marquee. The customers are willing to share more and more information about themselves with the hotel because their stay will be more relaxing and refreshing. Some people in marketing circles call this willingness of customers to divulge increasing amounts of personal information as an "opt-in" personalization service.

- **Partnerships.** An organization may develop a vital and important relationship with one or more of its customers. This relationship is sometimes taken beyond the normal supplier relationship when both organizations can foresee developing a win-win relationship. For example, an organization might collaborate with its customers on product development or marketing efforts.

Finally, an organization can define its customer value proposition using its *image or brand name*.[7] Some brand names have a lot of value and are quite old (consider Coca-Cola™ or Pepsi™); other valuable brands are relatively new (for example, Google™ or Amazon. Com™).

The library district in London's East End decided to close seven traditional branch public libraries over time and replace them with seven radically new "Idea Stores." This was done in an attempt to create a new brand identity to change the general perception of the library as a quaint, outdated, and obsolete institution to one that is vibrant, relevant, and hip.[8]

The Financial Perspective

The "bottom line" for any for-profit company is to choose a set of strategies that deliver long-term shareholder value by increasing the growth of revenues (and profits) as well as providing its overall productivity, for example, improving its asset utilization. Thus a company's annual report presents information about market share, revenue growth, profitability, and so forth.

For libraries, governments, or nonprofit organizations, the "bottom line" should be effectiveness: the delivery of required or desired services in an efficient manner to its customers.

Integrating the Perspectives

The strength of the balanced scorecard is that it allows the organization to focus on identifying the impact of its strategies using each of the perspectives. That is, by using a logic model the organization is able to formulate a cause-and-effect relationship between the perspectives. For example, consider the normal balanced scorecard, as shown in Figure 1.3 (page 8). Four broad assumptions about the interrelationships are hypothesized in a general cause-and-effect scorecard.

The scorecard's strengh is demonstrated by its balance: showing how well you *have been* doing (lagging indicators), how well you *are* doing (current indicators), and *can expect* to do in the future (leading indicators). Using a balanced scorecard will assist an organization in focusing on the factors that create long-term value for its customers.

Research has validated the underlying structure of the scorecard. For example:

- Increased employee satisfaction leads to higher performance.

- Service quality correlates significantly with customer satisfaction.

- Rework and waste significantly affect performance.[9]

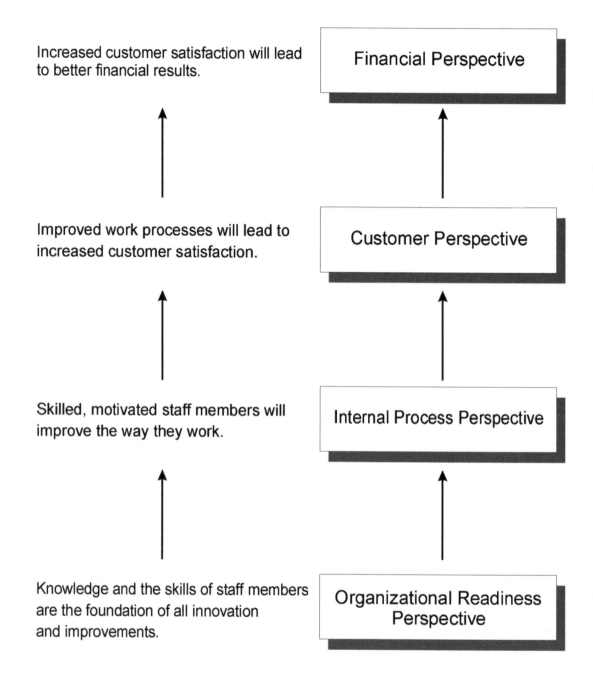

Increased customer satisfaction will lead to better financial results.

Financial Perspective

Improved work processes will lead to increased customer satisfaction.

Customer Perspective

Skilled, motivated staff members will improve the way they work.

Internal Process Perspective

Knowledge and the skills of staff members are the foundation of all innovation and improvements.

Organizational Readiness Perspective

Figure 1.3. Cause-and-Effect Relationships in the For-Profit Environment

8

Other Scorecards

Other scorecard models have been suggested, but none of these approaches has achieved anywhere near the popularity of the balanced scorecard.[10]

EXPERIENCES IN USING THE BALANCED SCORECARD

Because of its flexibility, the balanced scorecard has been used quite successfully by a large number of small to very large organizations in almost every sector of the economy. The framework of the scorecard provides the necessary structure, and the detail can be tailored to fit the needs of any organization. Often the results of introducing and using the balanced scorecard can be quite dramatic and very positive.

The use of a scorecard is not a one-time event, but rather must be integrated into the fabric of the organization so that it influences how people perform their jobs on a daily basis. The popularity of the balanced scorecard is attested to, in part, by the fact that the Balanced Scorecard Technology Council has more than 10,000 members.

Among some of the organizations that have adopted the use of the balanced scorecard are the following:

- **Service and Hospitality:** Hilton Hotels, United Parcel Service, Wendy's, and Marriott Vacation Club International

- **Financial Service:** Skandia, Mellon Bank, Cigna, Chemical Bank, and Wells Fargo

- **Health Care:** Duke Children's Hospital, Montefiore, and SIVDC

- **Education:** University of California Administrative Services on each campus and the Fulton County (GA) Schools

- **Police and Military:** U.S. Army, Royal Norwegian Air Force, UK Ministry of Defence, and the Royal Canadian Mounted Police

- **Government:** State (TX) Auditor's Office, City of Charlotte, North Carolina, and the City of Brisbane, Australia

- **Telecommunications:** Mobistar, GTE, AT&T Canada, and Crown Castle

- **Libraries:** The Singapore Public Libraries and the University of Virginia library

Organizations are using the scorecard to

- clarify, update, and communicate strategy;

- link strategic objectives to performance measures with associated long-term targets;

- broaden management's focus on issues that affect sustainable long-term performance;

- provide a focus for continuous process improvement efforts and quality enhancement initiatives;

- identify and align strategic initiatives;

- improve the quality of services;

- eliminate non-value-added activities;

- identify critical employee competencies;
- learn about what capabilities are critical to realizing strategic intent; and
- demonstrate accountability.

One of the primary reasons that the balanced scorecard has been so successful is that it assists an organization in translating its vision and strategies into concrete actions to be carried out by people throughout the organization. In short, the selection of the correct performance measures will show how well the organization is doing in terms of implementing its strategy. When used in this way, the scorecard becomes a strategic management tool rather than simply a new format for monitoring performance.

Strategic management is a systems approach to identifying and making the necessary changes and measuring the organization's performance as it moves toward its vision. Rather than merely being a collection of performance measures or a wish list for continuous improvement, the scorecard prescribes a plan for strategic execution.

The balanced scorecard approach can be adapted by organizations to meet their specific goals and circumstances. For example, one Swedish insurance company, the Skandia Group, believed that to succeed, the company had to build value through "intellectual capital." The company felt that it must build and leverage the value of intangible assets like customer relationships and unique computer software.[11] Skandia calls its version of the scorecard "navigator" and uses five perspectives or focuses: financial, customer, human, process, and renewal and development. The Skandia Navigator, shown in Figure 1.4, also provides a historical context for the structure of its scorecard.

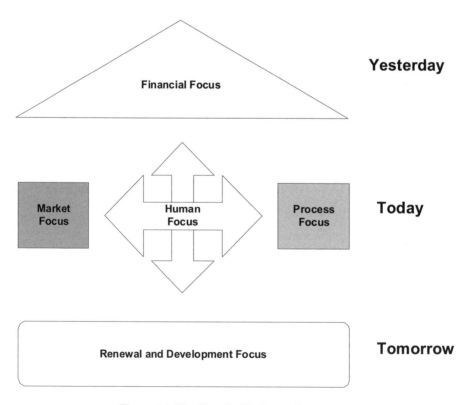

Figure 1.4. The Skandia Navigator Framework

The use of multidimensional perspectives found in a balanced scorecard will change the perception of the library's performance, *away* from past performance and *toward* what the library seeks to become.

The balanced scorecard, as shown in Figure 1.5 (page 12), assists the organization in answering two fundamental questions:

- What do we want to achieve, and what must we do to achieve it? (Illustrated in the top half of the figure.)

- Are we doing what we set out to do? (Illustrated by the bottom half of the figure.)

The balanced scorecard:

IS	IS NOT
A strategy-based management system	Just a performance measurement tool
A journey	A project
An organizational process requiring real effort	A "quick and easy" project
A change initiative	"Business as usual"
Balancing of nonfinancial, efficiency, infrastructure, and financial views of an organization	Placing existing performance measures into one of four "hoppers"
Increased accountability	Tighter control
Improving communication throughout the organization	Using measures as a control mechanism
Aligning operations with vision	A quality control or reengineering project

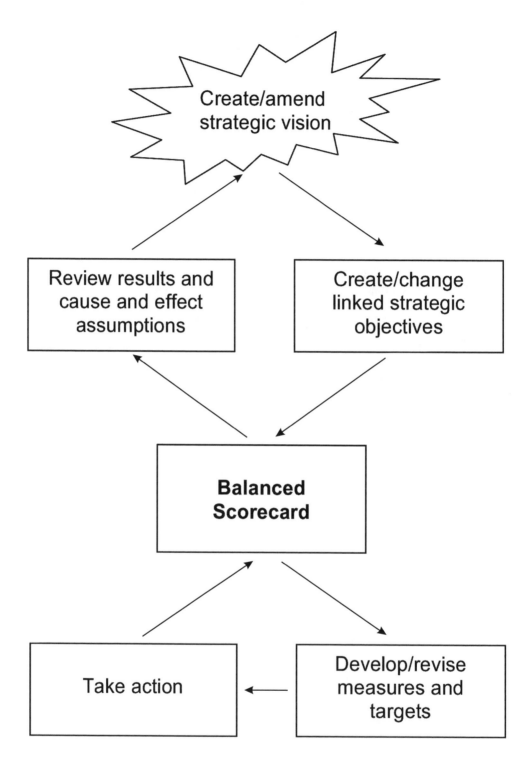

Figure 1.5. Balanced Scorecard Overview

12

ADDITIONAL RESOURCES

For additional information about scorecards, consult the following sources.

Hannabarger, Chuck, Rick Buchman, and Peter Economy. *Balanced Scorecard Strategy for Dummies.* Indianapolis, IN: Wiley, 2007.

Kaplan, Robert S., and David P. Norton. *The Strategy-Focused Organization.* Boston: Harvard Business School Press, 2001.

————. *Strategy Maps: Converting Intangible Assets into Tangible Outcomes.* Boston: Harvard Business School Press, 2004.

Niven, Paul R. *Balanced Scorecard Step-by-Step for Government and Nonprofit Agencies.* New York: Wiley, 2003.

Olve, Nils-Goran, Carl-Johan Petri, Jan Roy, and Sofie Roy. *Making Scorecards Actionable: Balancing Strategy and Control.* New York: Wiley, 2003.

The Society of Management Accountants of Canada. *Applying the Balanced Acorecard.* Mississauga, ON: The Society of Management Accountants of Canada, 1999.

For a discussion of the applicability of the balanced scorecard in libraries, consult the following sources.

Hallowell, Roger, and Lynda M. Applegate. *Transforming Singapore's Public Libraries (Abridged).* Case Study 9-802-028. Boston: Harvard Business School Press, 2004. 19 pages.

Hallowell, Roger, Carin-Isabel Knoop, and Neo Boon Siong. *Transforming Singapore's Public Libraries.* Case Study 9-802-009. Boston: Harvard Business School Press, 2001. 26 pages.

Matthews, Joseph R. "Balanced Scorecard in Public Libraries: A Project Summary." In *Proceedings of the Library Assessment Conference: Building Effective, Sustainable, Practical Assessment. September 25–27, 2006, Charlottesville, Virginia,* 293–302. Washington, DC: Association of Research Libraries, 2007.

————. "The Library Balanced Scorecard: Is It in Your Future?" *Public Libraries* 45, no. 6 (November/December 2006): 64–71.

————. *Measuring for Results: The Dimensions of Public Library Effectiveness.* Westport, CT: Libraries Unlimited, 2004. Chapter 9.

Poll, Roswitha. "Performance, Processes and Costs: Managing Service Quality with the Balanced Scorecard." *Library Trends* 49, no. 4 (Spring 2001): 709–17.

Self, James. "From Values to Metrics: Implementation of the Balanced Scorecard at the University Library." *Performance Measurement & Metrics* 4, no. 2 (2003): 57–63.

————. "Metrics and Management: Applying the Results of the Balanced Scorecard." *Performance Measurement and Metrics* 5, no. 3 (2004): 101–5.

————. "Using Data to Make Choices: The Balanced Scorecard at the University of Virginia Library." *ARL* 230/231 (October/November 2003): 28–29.

For more resources, see the appendix.

RELATED WEB SITES

- The **Library Balanced Scorecard Project** maintains a Web site that includes a tutorial and other resources: http://www.ci.carlsbad.ca.us/imls.

- The **Balanced Scorecard Institute** (http://www.balancedscorecard.org/) is an independent educational institute that provides training and guidance to assist government agencies and companies in applying best practices in balanced scorecard (BSC) and performance measurement for strategic management and transformation.

- The **Balanced Scorecard Interest Group** (BaSIG) (http://www.balancedscorecardsurvival. com/) is hosted by the American Society for Public Administration and the National Academy for Public Administration. Its meetings take place in Washington, D.C. The Balanced Scorecard Interest Group has two goals:

  - Help organizations that are contemplating the use of balanced scorecards obtain the information they need to make informed decisions.

  - Help organizations that have decided to design and install a balanced scorecard learn from the experiences of others.

- The **Federal Library and Information Center Committee**, located in Washington, D.C, has a streaming video of a presentation entitled "Program Evaluation: The Balanced Scorecard Method," which is available at http://loc.gov/flicc/video/balance/balancedscore.html.

- The **Palladium Group** (http://www.thepalladiumgroup.com/pages/welcome.aspx/) is a for-profit professional consulting firm that facilitates the worldwide awareness, use, enhancement, and integrity of the balanced scorecard (BSC) as a value-added management process. The firm was created by Robert Kaplan and David Norton, the originators of the balanced scorecard.

- The **University of Virginia Library** has some background information about the balanced scorecard as well as links to the measures that the library has selected, available at http://www.lib.virginia.edu/bsc/.

- The **University of California at Berkeley** Business and Administrative Services has developed a scorecard and provide an explanation of its scorecard at http://bas.berkeley.edu/BalancedScorecard/Home.htm.

- The **University of California at San Diego** also has developed a scorecard, available at http://www-vcba.ucsd.edu/PerfMeas/toc.htm.

- The **California State University, San Marcos** Finance & Administrative Services has an excellent Web site for its balanced scorecard activities, including a tutorial (also includes links to other CSU campuses that have scorecard initiatives), at http://www.csusm.edu/bsc.

NOTES

1. Colin B. Carter and Jay W. Lorsch, *Back to the Drawing Board – Designing Corporate Boards for a Complex World* (Boston: Harvard Business School Press, 2004).

2. The balanced scorecard was first introduced in a *Harvard Business Review* article that appeared in January 1992. A series of articles by Kaplan and Norton appeared over the following years further expanding and explaining the scorecard concepts.

3. Monica Franco and Mike Bourne. "Factors That Play a Role in 'Managing Through Measures'." *Management Decision* 41, no. 8 (2003): 698–710.

4. Michael Hammer and James Champy, *Reengineering the Corporation: A Manifesto for Business Revolution* (New York: HarperBusiness, 1993). See also David Osborne and Ted Gaebler, *Reinventing Government: How the Entrepreneurial Spirit Is Transforming the Public Sector* (New York: Addison-Wesley, 1992).

5. Joseph R. Matthews, *The Evaluation and Measurement of Library Services* (Westport, CT: Libraries Unlimited, 2007).

6. Calvin N. Mooers, "Mooers' Law or, Why Some Retrieval Systems Are Used and Others Are Not," *American Documentation* 11 (1960): 204.

7. Neeli Bendapudi and Venkat Bendapudi, "Creating the Living Brand," *Harvard Business Review* 83, no. 5 (May 2005): 124–32.

8. Thomas Patterson, "Idea Stores: London' New Libraries," *Library Journal* 126, no. 8 (May 1, 2001): 48–49.

9. James R. Evans and Eric P. Jack. Validating Key Results Linkages in the Baldridge Performance Excellence Model. *Quality Management Journal*, 10 (2), April 2003, 7–26.

10. See, for example, Steve Montague, *The Three Rs of Performance: Core Concepts for Planning, Measurement, and Management* (Ottawa: Performance Management Network, 1997); Andy Neely, Chris Adams, and Mike Kennerley, *The Performance Prism: The Scorecard for Measuring and Managing Business Success* (London: Prentice Hall, 2002); Andy Neely and Chris Adams, "The Performance Prism Perspective," *Journal of Cost Management* 15, no. 1 (January/February 2001): 7–15; Andy Neely, Chris Adams, and Paul Crowe, "The Performance Prism in Practice," *Measuring Business Excellence* 5, no. 2 (2001): 6–12. Information about The Big Picture Framework is available at http://www.thbigpic.org.uk.

11. Leif Edvinsson and Michael S. Malone, *Intellectual Capital: Realizing Your Company's True Value by Finding Its Hidden Roots* (New York: HarperCollins, 1997).

2

The Library Scorecard

The scorecard has clarified and focused our thinking. It has made us figure out what areas are important, and what constitutes success in those areas. We now look beyond customer service, realizing that success in other categories (finance, processes, the future) ultimately improves service to our customers.

—Jim Self[1]

Libraries are no strangers to the gathering, collection, and reporting of a plethora of performance measures. Some of these measures are gathered as the result of tradition; some are mandated by a state library; and others are the remnants of actions undertaken by prior library directors. Most library performance measures collected each year can be classified as input and output measures.

Historically, the vast majority of performance measures have had a control bias for all types and sizes of organizations. That is, the effect of a performance measurement system is to indicate the particular actions management wants its employees to take. The performance measures are then used to determine the extent to which employees are acting according to plan.

The balanced scorecard focuses not on control but rather on the organization's vision and strategies. Once the performance measures have been identified and targets or goals selected, the scorecard process assumes that people will adopt whatever behavior and take whatever actions are necessary to help achieve those goals. The focus has changed from the traditional priority of programs and initiatives to the balanced scorecards emphasis on vision and goals.

Despite its origins in assisting for-profit companies in selecting, implementing, and tracking their progress as they work to achieve their visions, the balanced scorecard has been successfully extended for use in both government and nonprofit organizations. Robert Kaplan, who helped develop the balanced scorecard, has suggested an alternative scorecard format for nonprofit organizations, shown in Figure 2.1 (page 18). A slight modification of the balanced scorecard shown in Figure 2.1 adds a "public value and benefit perspective," as shown in Figure 2.2 (page 19).

17

The Business and Administrative Services Unit of the University of California—Berkeley, has revised the original scorecard into another effective format, as shown in Figure 2.3 (page 20).

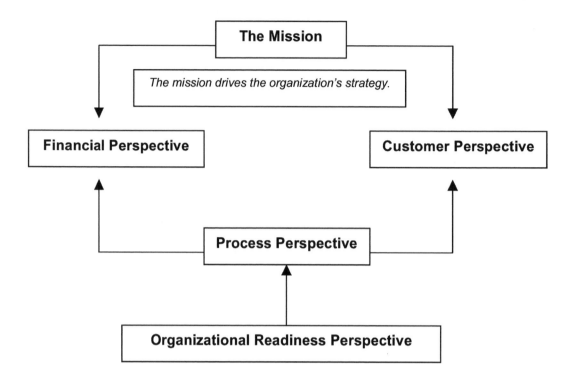

Figure 2.1. Balanced Scorecard for Nonprofit Organizations. Adapted from Robert S. Kaplan, "Strategic Performance Measurement and Management in Nonprofit Organizations," *Nonprofit Management & Leadership* 11, no. 3 (Spring 2001): 353–70.

Although the four traditional perspectives of the original scorecard can be adequate, they frequently need relabeling to have relevance. Alternative labels could be the following:

- **Impact:** focusing on the impact that the service is trying to have on its customers and its community

- **Service management:** focusing on how well managed the key activities or processes are that are important for effective service delivery

- **Resource management:** focusing on how well resources are being acquired or used.

- **Improvement** focusing on the actions or initiatives intended to deliver service improvements.[2]

Another alternative relabeling of the perspectives includes the following:

- Performance focus

- Relationship focus

- Activity focus

- Future focus

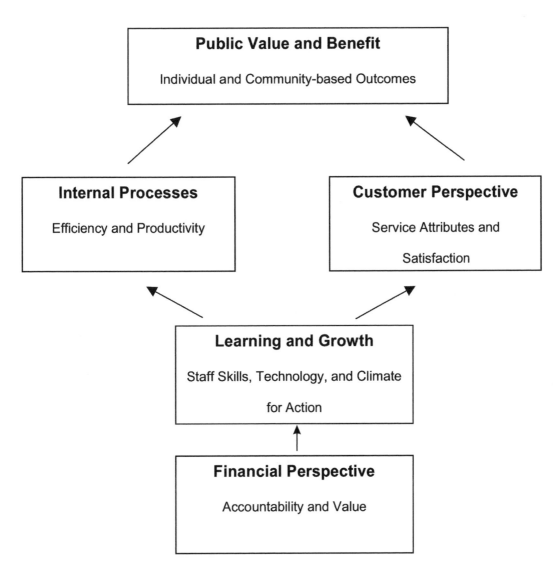

Figure 2.2. Public Value and Benefit Scorecard

19

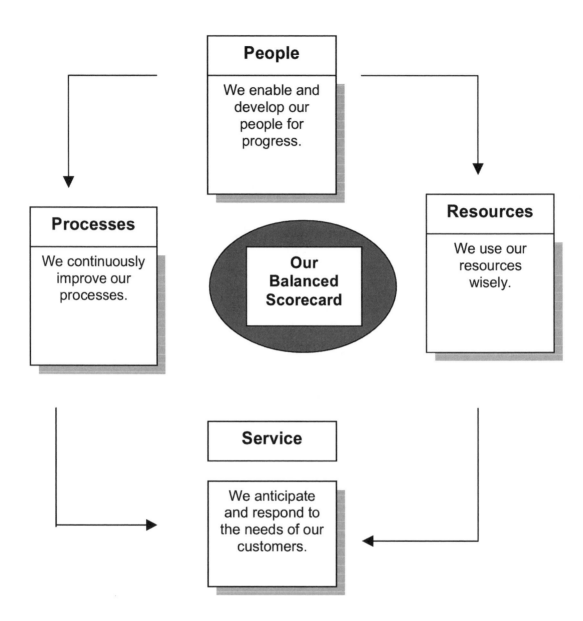

Figure 2.3. University of California–Berkeley Balanced Scorecard

Because a library is not like other organizations in many ways, it may be appropriate for it to utilize one or more additional perspectives as it develops its own library balanced scorecard. For example, the library might want to consider an additional perspective labeled the *Information Resources Perspective*.[3] A library's information resources perspective comprises the physical resources or collection of materials, access to electronic databases licensed by the library, selected high-quality Web resources (links might be contained in the library's catalog or on its Web site), as well as resources obtained from other sources using interlibrary loan or document delivery.

A potential model for a library balanced scorecard is shown in Figure 2.4.

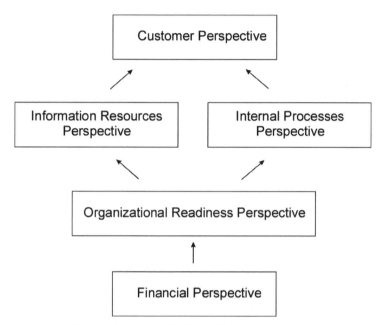

Figure 2.4. Suggested Library Balanced Scorecard

"Reading" the scorecard is fairly straightforward. Start at the bottom and work your way up. A lower perspective is the driver or enabler of the perspective above—the outcome.

Starting at the bottom of the strategy map, the financial perspective identifies the financial and other resources provided to the library (with measures to indicate that the funds received are well spent) used to ensure that skilled staff and the necessary information technology infrastructure are in place (organizational readiness perspective).

Placing the financial perspective at the bottom seems appropriate, as most libraries are not in the "for-profit" arena and use their budgetary resources to drive the delivery of services.

Staff members use the available tools in an efficient manner (internal processes perspective), and the library continues to provide access to appropriate collection materials and online resources (information resources perspective). This combination of skilled staff, information resources, and efficient processes should deliver the correct mix of products and services that are highly valued by the library's customers (the customer perspective)—if the library has a good understanding of the needs of its customers and it has selected the appropriate strategies to meet those needs. As shown in Figure 2.5 (page 22), developing, using, adjust, and updating a scorecard is an ongoing process.

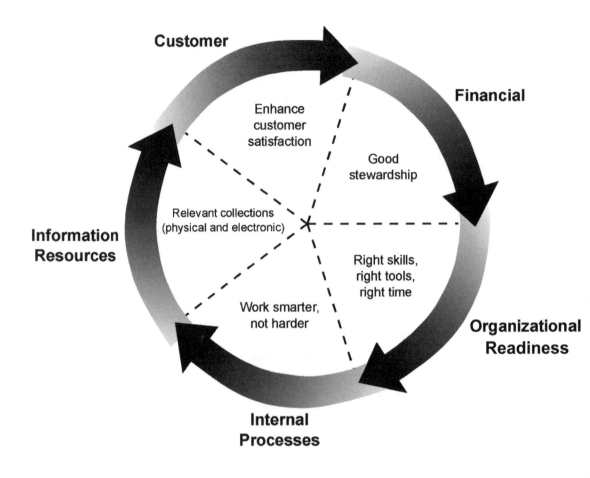

Customer

Financial

Enhance
customer
satisfaction

Good
stewardship

**Information
Resources**

Relevant collections
(physical and electronic)

Right skills,
right tools,
right time

Work smarter,
not harder

**Organizational
Readiness**

**Internal
Processes**

Figure 2.5 The Library Balanced Scorecard

For the scorecard approach to have real value for a specific library, the resulting scorecard must

- reflect the specific services, strategies, service responses, vision, and values of the library;
- have a logical cause-and-effect relationship among the perspectives that can be easily and clearly communicated to the library's stakeholders;
- not be seen as a one-time event, but rather as a change process that will require ongoing attention and management; and
- be built by a cooperative team of people, acknowledge that the process to develop a scorecard is very collaborative, and acknowledge that adjustments, changes, and modifications will occur throughout the process.

In summation, the library will have to decide how many perspectives to employ for its scorecard and how these perspectives are related to one another in a logical manner. The structure of the scorecard will, in effect, tell the story of how the library delivers value to its customers. The process of creating a scorecard will document the following:

- **What** you are trying to accomplish
- **How** you plan to do it (your strategy)
- How you will **manage** success

Ultimately, the stakeholders want the library to deliver quality services that yield good results in a cost-effective manner. The library balanced scorecard can be an important tool in demonstrating the value of the library to its community.

NOTES

1. James Self, "Metrics and Management: Applying the Results of the Balanced Scorecard," *Performance Measurement & Metrics* 5, no. 3 (2004): 101–5.

2. Mik Wisniewski and Snjolfur Olafsson, "Developing Balanced Scorecards in Local Authorities: A Comparison of Experience," *International Journal of Productivity and Performance Management* 53, no. 7 (2004): 602–10.

3. Joseph R. Matthews, *Measuring for Results: The Dimensions of Public Library Effectiveness* (Westport, CT: Libraries Unlimited, 2004).

3

A Suggested Process

> *The balanced scorecard is NOT about "the right measures." Rather, it is a process and culture for choosing, using, and revising measures to assist the library to focus on achieving its vision.*

The challenge for any organization, including a library, is to figure out answers to five very important questions:

- **Why?** Why does the organization exist?
- **Where?** Where is the organization headed (the vision thing!)?
- **Who?** Who are its customers?
- **What?** What are its product and service offerings?
- **How?** How will the organization create and deliver its products and services (the strategies to be employed)?

Using a top-down approach, an organization is able to link its mission and vision to the strategies that it will use to achieve its vision (see Figure 3.1, page 26).

DETERMINE WHO PARTICIPATES

The library director will need to appoint staff members to the balanced scorecard team. Normally the team should include five to nine individuals who will work well together and have the ability to view the library from a broader perspective. Involving individuals from all levels and departments of the organization will provide a variety of perspectives, which will be beneficial. Clearly developing a library balanced scorecard is something new for your library, which will involve asking lots of questions and challenging a long-standing list of assumptions about what constitutes a library.

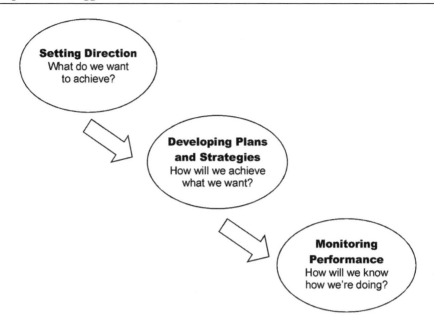

Figure 3.1. Aligning the Mission, the Vision, Strategies, and Measurement

The library director should appoint a scorecard team leader who will assume responsibility for scheduling meetings and creating documents and other materials. Most important, the team leader will be an advocate for the library's balanced scorecard. It is vital that the team leader read extensively in order to serve as a "mentor" or "coach" for the team as it works to develop the library's scorecard.

> **Tip!** Remember that developing a library balanced scorecard is a multiyear commitment. The scorecard will have to be updated quarterly, and the process of developing the scorecard will likely require a number of projects and initiatives that will need resources, management attention, and follow-up.

Larger libraries may want to create an action team for each perspective. The benefits of such an approach are that a larger group of people will become familiar with the concept of a balanced scorecard and a broader cross-section of knowledgeable staff members will be involved in selecting strategies and the associated performance measures.

WHO WILL FACILITATE

The library should carefully consider the important role of facilitator. The facilitator may be an outside consultant or a staff member. If the facilitator is a staff member, he or she will have to invest a fair amount of time to become more knowledgeable about the concept of balanced scorecards.

The facilitator's role is to both be a resource person about balanced scorecards and encourage and suggest alternatives to the team responsible for developing and implementing the scorecard in the library.

UNDERSTANDING THE STAKEHOLDERS' PERSPECTIVE

Prior to embarking on the process to develop your library's balanced scorecard, it is key to your success to arrange a meeting with a number of the library's funding decision makers and other interested stakeholders. This will help you better understand their perspective and experience with the concept of evaluating programs and services provided by public agencies in general and assessing the value of the local library in particular.

Some individuals are comfortable with the use of performance measures and statistics, whereas others rely more on qualitative information—reports of problems and frustrations being experienced by those who use the library as well as stories of people who are pleased with the local library. It is crucial to decide how they determine the value of various services, and more important, how they determine the value of your library. Are they interested in usage information (outputs), efficiency, impacts on library customers, and so forth? Having this information about how stakeholders view the use of performance measures and what they might like to see reported about how well the library is doing provides a foundation for all subsequent activities.

TIME COMMITMENT

Most organizations develop their balanced scorecard by meeting weekly in a two- to three-hour session. Because the topics involved in developing the library's scorecard are very important, care must be taken that the meetings are not interrupted.

Other organizations have used a much more intensive process, in which the scorecard team meets off-site for four to six days of intensive meetings. This latter approach will in most cases require the use of a facilitator to ensure that the team does not get sidetracked onto various tangential issues.

BUDGET IMPACT

The library should allocate a small amount of money to cover the purchase of materials, duplicating the scorecard, making posters, and so forth. Once the scorecard has been finalized, it will be necessary to make adjustments in the current budget to accommodate the initiatives and projects that will assist the library in achieving its goals.

THE PROCESS

The process to develop a balanced scorecard is fairly straightforward and incorporates elements of traditional strategic planning and the use of selected performance measures. This six-step process is outlined n in Figure 3.2. Each of the steps is explained in greater detail in the following chapters of this workbook.

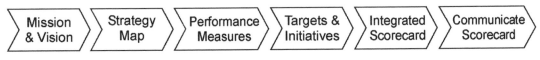

Figure 3.2. Six-Step Process

Step 1: Review the Library's Mission and Vision Statements

The development of a library's balanced scorecard starts with an abbreviated planning process that re-examines the library's mission statement and vision statement. The mission statement articulates the reason why the library exists, for whom it exists, and what products and services will be provided. The vision statement clarifies the long-term view of what the library will be at some point in the future.

Step 2: Develop a Strategy Map

Strategies are the means by which a library attempts to close the gap between what the library is today and its vision for the future. Another way to describe strategy is that it translates what customers want into what we must deliver!

This step begins by the library deciding upon which perspectives to include in its scorecard and its strategy map. The purpose of the strategy map is to visually illustrate the strategies that a library has chosen and the relationships that exist between each of the different perspectives in the library's scorecard.

Step 3: Select Performance Measures

A balanced scorecard contains a maximum of three to five performance measures for each perspective. Thus, the choice of each measure must be carefully considered from a list of other potential measures that might be used. It is also important that the measures selected reflect in some way the strategies that the library has chosen to utilize. Also, employing a variety of types of measures—input, process, outputs, and outcomes or result measures—has been proven beneficial.

One important activity that can assist in the process of performance measurement selection is to identify the critical success factors for each perspective. A critical success factor is essential to the success of the library and distinguishes the library from its competitors.[1]

Some of the critical success factors for a library follow:

Responsive service	Quality service
Consistent service	Availability of information resources
Reliable information technology	Quality of staff
Staff skills	Staff attitudes
Working efficiently	Working effectively
Knowing the customer	Top management support
Communication program	Number of program offerings
Quality of library catalog	Display of materials
Usability of library Web site	

Having an unambiguous understanding of the critical success factors for each perspective will make clearer what performance measures should ultimately be selected.

Step 4: Identify Targets and Initiatives

This step establishes targets (both short-term and long-term—the length to be decided by the library) for each performance measure. The targets for each measure should be achievable yet still require a significant effort to reach the desired goals. In some cases, it may be necessary for the library to identify some of the initiatives required to achieve the targets for some of the measures.

Step 5: Integrate the Library Scorecard

Once the library has created its balanced scorecard, it then can become a focus of management meetings as well as departmental staff meetings. The scorecard affords the library the opportunity to move from a traditional management orientation toward problem solving by "fighting fires" and "juggling multiple balls simultaneously" to one of strategic management.

The library may also wish to cascade the scorecard down to the library's departments and branches. Using the balanced scorecard as the focus, the library will be able to more easily prioritize initiatives and projects. The library should also integrate the balanced scorecard into its annual budgeting process. That is, the strategic priorities identified in the scorecard can be used to help allocate the library's precious resources.

When executed well, the balanced scorecard process will assist a library in moving ahead to embrace a culture of assessment. With appropriate training and encouragement from the library's management team, staff members can assume responsibility for identifying problems, suggesting ways to gather data to perform an analysis, and make recommendations for improving existing library processes.

Step 6: Communicate the Library Balanced Scorecard

The library must choose how to present the results of the scorecard to its stakeholders from among several options. Generally, some text accompanies the scorecard, explaining the structure and cause-and-effect relationships among the perspectives. In most cases the library's balanced scorecard is updated on a quarterly basis (although some measures may be updated less frequently).

The comparison of each of the performance measures with its associated targets is typically displayed in a color-coded format similar to a traffic signal—green to indicate that the results exceed the target, yellow to signify that the results fell a little short of the target, and red to show that the results are significantly less than the desired target.

The scorecard is then shared with all library staff members as well as the interested stakeholders. Some organizations have developed a systematic communication program to share the results with everyone by posting the scorecard on their Web site, creating posters and placing them in the offices, including scorecard articles in a monthly staff newsletter, and so forth.

IMPLEMENTATION PROBLEMS

Introducing a balanced scorecard into any organization may be problematic and may fail for a variety of reasons. Among these are the following:

- The library director and the top management team do not see the value of, and are not committed to using, the scorecard as a management tool.

- The scorecard is seen as a one-time event and not a part of the management system.

- The scorecard is not introduced to library staff members using an ongoing communication program to inform them of the benefits and seek their comments and reactions.

- The scorecard is viewed as only a visual aid for the collection of a variety of performance measures.

- There is a failure to recognize that the scorecard will involve change and that change management techniques should be used.

- The scorecard is built by one person or a very small team, with no involvement among top management of the library.

SUMMARY

The library balanced scorecard has the potential to transform a library by clearly communicating the library's strategies, performance measures, targets, and initiatives to staff members so that they can more closely align their day-to-day activities to achieve the library's vision, as shown in Figure 3.3. The scorecard is also valuable in communicating to stakeholders what the library is all about.

NOTES

1. Mark Graham Brown, *Winning Score: How to Design and Implement Organizational Scorecards* (Portland, OR: Productivity, 2001).

| **Mission** |
| *Why we exist* |

| **Vision** |
| *What we want to be* |

| **Strategy** |
| *How we will get there* |

| **Balanced Scorecard** |
| *Focus, align, and measure progress* |

| **Strategic Initiatives** |
| *What the priorities are* |

| **Strategic Outcomes** |

| Delighted **CUSTOMERS** | Efficient **PROCESSES** | Prepared **ORGANIZATION** | Informed **STAKEHOLDERS** |

Figure 3.3. Why a Library Should Use a Balanced Scorecard

4

Step 1: The Mission and Vision

A library's mission statement provides answers to some very important questions: Why does the library exist? Whom does the library serve? What services are provided? What makes the library distinctive or unique? In short, the mission statement defines the core purpose of the library—its raison d'être.

A mission statement that is clear and understandable clarifies the role of the library for any interested party, whether staff member or stakeholder in its community. As David Osborne and Ted Gaebler have noted:

> The experience of hashing out the fundamental purpose of an organization—debating all the different assumptions and views held by its members and agreeing on one basic mission—can be a powerful one. When it is done right, a mission statement can drive an entire organization from top to bottom.[1]

The mission statement must demonstrate the difference an organization will make for those it serves, rather than merely describing what the library does. It describes **WHY** the library exists, not what methods are used to deliver its services. Your mission statement should be broad enough to allow for growth and expansion, but narrow enough to keep the library driven and clearly focused.

There is no reason to expect that just compiling and displaying a mission, vision, and core values will change how people act (although this is a practice of many organizations). Yet some managers act as if these statements have magical powers to satisfy customers, increase quality, and make employees more productive and happy. Eileen Shapiro has suggested that one definition of a mission statement is "a talisman, hung in public places, to ward off evil spirits."[2]

USEFUL MISSION STATEMENTS

Figure 4.1 (page 34) provides some sample mission statements from some of America's better known companies. Can you identify the name of the company by reading its mission statement? Figure 4.2 (page 35) contains some sample public library mission statements, and Figure 4.3 (page 36) provides some sample academic library mission statements.

A   To solve unsolved problems innovatively.

B   To give unlimited opportunity to women.

C   To preserve and improve human life.

D   To give ordinary folk the chance to buy the same thing as rich people.

E   To make people happy.

F   We are a global family with a proud heritage, passionately committed to providing personal mobility for people around the world.

G   To organize the world's information and make it universally accessible and useful.

H   We want to be the best service organization in the world.

I   We will produce outstanding financial returns by providing totally reliable, competitively superior, global, air-ground transportation of high-priority goods and documents that require rapid, time-certain delivery.

J   Become the company most known for changing the worldwide poor-quality image of Japanese products.

K   Solve complex network computing problems for governments, enterprises, and service providers.

L   Our mission is to earn the loyalty of XXX owners and grow our family by developing and marketing U.S.-manufactured vehicles that are world leaders in quality, cost, and customer enthusiasm through the integration of people, technology, and business systems.

M   We sell soda.

N   We bring good things to life.

P   Dedication to the highest quality of customer service delivered with a sense of warmth, friendliness, individual pride, and Company Spirit.

Figure 4.1 Sample Mission Statements

A = 3M, B = Mary Kay Cosmetics, C = Merck, D = Wal-Mart, E = Walt Disney, F = Ford Motor Company, G = Google, H = IBM, I = FedEx, J = Sony (in the 1950s), K = Sun Microsystems, L = Saturn, M = Pepsi, N = GE, P = Southwest Airlines

A crucible of ideas. A place where magic happens. Explore. Dream. Discover. Soar. We are your Library.—Ramsey County Library, MN

A vital and dynamic community resource that promotes lifelong learning.—The Cleveland Heights-University Heights Public Library

We help people achieve their full potential.—Denver Public Library

The Indianapolis-Marion County Public Library is an essential community information service providing materials and programs in support of the lifelong learning, recreational and economic interests of all citizens of Marion County.

The public library offers free and equal access to services and resources to assist the people of Montgomery County in finding ideas and information to sustain and enrich their lives.

The mission of the Fairfax County Public Library is to enrich individual and community life by providing and encouraging the use of library resources and services to meet the evolving educational, recreational and informational needs of the residents of Fairfax County and Fairfax City.

Hennepin County Library promotes full and equal access to information and ideas, the love of reading, the joy of learning, and engagement with the arts, sciences and humanities.

The mission of the Salt Lake County Library System is to make a positive difference in the lives of our customers by responsively providing materials, information, and services at community libraries located throughout the Salt Lake Valley and/or via the Library's World Wide Web site.

We promote reading and guide learning in the pursuit of information, knowledge and wisdom.—Columbus Metropolitan Library, OH

The community connection to reading, lifelong learning and personal and professional enrichment for people of all ages.—Greene County Public Library System

Figure 4.2. Sample Public Library Mission Statements

The Georgetown University Library is an agile organization that respects the heritage of the past while anticipating the requirements of the 21st-century. By providing preeminent services, collections and spaces, the Library shapes the creation of knowledge, conserves culture for posterity, and transforms learning and research.

The University of Oregon Libraries enriches the student learning experience, encourages exploration and research at all levels, and contributes to advancements in access to scholarly resources.

The mission of the University Library at Cal State Hayward is to provide user-focused quality services and collections in support of undergraduate and graduate programs, faculty research, and the general information needs of the diverse community. The University Library provides access to recorded knowledge in all formats regardless of ownership. Consistent with the teaching mission of the university, the library assists students in becoming information competent, critical thinkers, and life-long learners. The University Library provides physical facilities to foster individual and collaborative teaching and learning and to encourage the exchange of ideas.

The University of Illinois at Chicago (UIC) Library strives to meet the information needs of UIC students, faculty, and staff. The library contributes to teaching, research, outreach, and clinical service at UIC by acquiring, organizing, and archiving information and by providing expert staff, access to information sources in all formats, and instruction in the retrieval and use of information. The UIC Library also extends information services through a variety of cooperative and reciprocal programs, regionally, nationally, and internationally. The library faculty conducts research that addresses the theoretical and practical aspects of information organization, preservation, retrieval, and delivery.

The mission of the University of Delaware Library is to gather, organize, preserve, and provide access to the information resources necessary for the University of Delaware to achieve its educational, research, and service goals.

The Yale University Library, as one of the world's leading research libraries, collects, organizes, preserves, and provides access to and services for a rich and unique record of human thought and creativity. It fosters intellectual growth and supports the teaching and research missions of Yale University and scholarly communities worldwide.

Figure 4.3. Sample Academic Library Mission Statements

Some of the attributes of a useful mission statement are that they are:

- **Simple and clear.** Even a cursory examination of a few library mission statements will clearly make the point that most library mission statements want to be all things for all people! This desire means there is a lack of focus that will result in poor services. Peter Drucker calls this mistake an attempt to turn missions into "hero sandwiches of good intentions."[3]

    A mission statement must be articulated in one or two sentences. Anything more obviates the requirement to be simple and clear. If the library's mission statement won't fit on a T-shirt, then it's too long! Similarly, the statement must avoid the use of any library jargon.

- **Broad and long-term in nature.** Although the service offerings, strategies, and tactics of the library may change, the mission statement should be as valid 20 years from now as it is today.

- **Focused on the present.** The library mission statement should not be future oriented—that is the role of the vision statement.

- **Easy to understand.** If the mission statement is easy to understand, then it will be easy to communicate to the library's staff members, key stakeholders, as well as to the community at large. A compelling mission statement will not resort to buzz words—such words typically have a very short shelf life.

Quick test! Check your library's existing mission statement. What grade would you assign your statement using the above criteria? Perhaps it is time to revisit and revise your library's mission statement!

WRITING A MISSION STATEMENT

One useful approach to creating or updating your library's mission statement s to use the following template.

We exist to *(purpose or need)*
_____
to provide *(services or products)*
_____
for *(customers)*
_____
so that *(planned outcomes or benefits)*
_____

After you have revised the library's mission statement, make sure it is reviewed by staff members at all levels as well as by stakeholders, and work to embrace any concerns that may arise. The mission statement must serve to inform all staff members and other stakeholders about the central focus of the library.[4]

Prior to drafting its mission statement, the library may want to consider and identify its core competency, as suggested by Gary Hamel and C. K. Prahalad.[5] A "core competency" is what is at the heart of an organization and defines in a major way the customer value proposition or the benefits that a customer experiences. Having a clear understanding of the library's competencies will determine, in part, the choice of the broad strategies selected by the library.

For the vast majority of libraries, the core competency is likely to be the library's collections—both physical and electronic. The Delaware State Library defined the core purpose of a public library as, "Collections available to Inform, Educate, and Entertain."

Note that the mission and the library's core values will remain fairly stable over time. The library's vision provides a picture of the future that clarifies the library's direction and helps staff members understand why and how they should support the library. The mission statement should also be very readable.[6]

THE VISION STATEMENT

A *vision* describes a desired future state or set of circumstances. It is brief and provides a picture of the future as seen through the eyes of the *customers*, *stakeholders,* and *employees*. A vision statement translates the library's mission into intended results. A good vision will assist the library in formulating strategies and objectives as well as allocating resources.

A good vision statement will not only inspire and challenge, but also be meaningful so that staff members will be able to relate their jobs to the vision. The vision should be broad, enduring, and "grab your heart." It provides direction and contributes to a library's identity and uniqueness. It inspires action that leads to achieving results. And most important, the vision statement must be *measurable* in some way so that the library will know if it is making progress toward achieving its vision.

Stephen Covey, in *The Seven Habits of Highly Effective People*, exhorts managers to always "Begin with the end in mind." Accordingly, the library should be asking the following questions:

- What is it that the library wants to do?

- What are we hoping to accomplish?
- What results are we seeking?
- How will we enhance the quality of life for those who use our services?
- What do customers do at the library that they don't want to do?
- What are customers experiencing that they'd rather not?
- What do customers dream about doing, knowing, or experiencing?
- What inhibits potential customers from using the (physical or virtual) library?

Answering the question "Who is our customer?" provides the basis for determining what customers value, formulating the library's vision, and defining your results.

Customers change constantly. There will be greater or lesser numbers in the groups the library already serves. They will become more diverse. Their needs, wants, and aspirations will evolve. Does your library really know and understand the different segments that constitute its customer base? One helpful exercise to better understand the library's customers is to create Table 4.1, using the following guidelines:

- Make a list of the service attributes that are important to your customers. (You may need to create several tables to represent different customer segments.)
- Grade how well the library performs each attribute by asking a sample of your customers (use a 1–10 scale, with 10 being great).
- Grade how well you think the library's competitors perform, using the same 1–10 scale.[7]

The results should identify any mismatches between customer requirements and how well the library is performing.

Table 4.1. Customer Needs Analysis

Attributes	Customer Importance Rating	Library Performance	Competitor Performance
Collection had what I was looking for			
Adequate copies of popular materials			
Knowledgeable and competent staff			
Professional and friendly staff			
Welcoming library facility			
Did not need to wait in long lines			
Staff went the extra mile to get what I was looking for			
Programs have appealing and timely topics			
Information technology is reliable and fast			

Attributes shown in table are meant to be illustrative, not exhaustive.

Customer expectations about the library and its services are also changing, in some cases quite rapidly, as illustrated in Table 4.2.

Table 4.2 Old and New Views of the Library

Old Views	New Views
One model of library—size may vary	Market driven—different services at different locations
Custodian of books	Service-oriented information provider
Print predominates	Multimedia
Physical collection	Electronic collection
Go to library	Library comes to you
In good time	Just-in-time
Local reach	Global reach
Free basic service	Value-added services

USEFUL VISION STATEMENTS

As is the case when developing a mission statement, creating a vision statement can be a challenging assignment. Among the characteristics of an effective vision statement are the following:

- **Succinctness.** A really good vision statement immediately draws you in and captures your attention. If you must read a paragraph or two, then it will not be memorable or compelling. Much like a mission statement, the vision statement must be short enough to fit on a T-shirt.

- **Appeal.** The vision statement must paint a clear and compelling word picture about the future that will excite and energize all who are interested in the library—staff members, stakeholders, and customers.

- **Feasibility.** The vision, with resources, energy, dedication, and time, must ultimately be achievable. The vision should involve setting some goals and objectives that will require the library and its staff members to stretch in order to achieve them. And it may well take 10 or more years to achieve, for example, President John F. Kennedy's vision of reaching the moon in a decade was designed to motivate and energize NASA as well as the nation.

- **Meaningfulness.** The library's leadership team must walk the walk and not simply talk the talk in order to demonstrate that the vision has real meaning. How the management allocates time and resources will clearly demonstrate whether the vision is embraced "heart and soul." A good vision statement will engender a positive emotional response, but vision statements should not use words that describe an emotion.

- **Measurability.** The vision statement should contain language that will make it possible to develop performance measures that assist the library in determining when the vision has been realized or achieved. For example, Microsoft's vision statement in its early years was, "A desktop PC in every office and home." Because the number of homes and offices is known, it is possible to measure the progress that being made toward that vision.

As can be seen in Figure 4.4 (page 42), some organizations have developed vision statements that convey a lot—sometimes with very few words. Can you identify each company after reading its vision statement? An interesting exception to the short vision statement is Sony's, which uses a series of short sentences to convey a very forceful vision. Figure 4.5 (page 43) provides some sample public library vision statements, and Figure 4.6 (page 44) contains some sample academic library vision statements.

The vision statement must recognize the environment within which the organization operates—that is, that change is constant and that competitors exist, even for your library. In developing a vision statement, a library should consider the following questions:

- Who are the library's primary customers?

- What are the library's priorities, as represented in the vision?

- What would the future look like if the goals were achieved and the vision fulfilled?

- What are the library's greatest opportunities in the future?

- How will the library enhance the quality of life for those who use its services and products?

- How does the library describe the desired future?

- What contribution to the community's quality of life will the library be making?

A   To be the most successful computer company in the world at delivering the best customer experience in markets we serve.

B   Empower people through great software anytime, anyplace, and on any device.

C   We will grow by helping our customer's win—through the ingenuity and responsiveness of people who care.

D   Everything and everyone connected to the network.

E   XXX is a company dedicated to the celebration of life.
>   We create things for every kind of imagination.
>   Products that stimulate the senses and refresh the spirit.
>   Ideas that always surprise, and never disappoint.
>   Innovations that are easy to love, and effortless to use.
>   Things that are not essential, but hard to live without.
>   We're not here to be logical. Or predictable.
>   We're here to pursue infinite possibilities.
>   We allow the brightest minds to interact freely, so the unexpected can emerge.
>   We invite new thinking, so even more fantastic ideas can evolve.
>   Creativity is our essence.
>   We take chances. We exceed expectations.
>   We help dreamers dream.

F   People working together as a global enterprise for aerospace leadership.

G   One can embrace either a static or a dynamic way of seeing the world. And this is followed by the brand's company ambition, which is "to be the catalyst of change for a whole generation."

H   To become the worldwide leader in retailing

I   The world's leading provider of hospitality services.

J   The perfect search engine would understand exactly what you mean and give back exactly what you want.

Figure 4.4. Sample Vision Statements

A = Dell Computer, B = Microsoft, C = 3M, D = Sun Microsystems, E = Sony, F = Boeing, G = Pepsi, H = Wal-Mart, I = Marriott, J = Google

Expanding our communities' possibilities by touching one mind at a time. BCPL: the best place to learn, to discover, to imagine, to smile.—Baltimore County Public Library

Montgomery County Public Libraries are the gateway for easy and equitable access to information, ideas and enrichment; where the lifelong learning needs of people are met by a diverse staff through traditional library services and new methods of information delivery; and where community needs and interests are understood in the planning and provision of all types of library services.

The Hennepin County Library staff, Board, and community envision a future where all individuals and families are eager and engaged lifelong learners.

Naperville Public Library–Naperville's Neighborhood of Knowledge is our community's top stop for equitable access to knowledge and information delivered by professional and welcoming staff in a network of state of the art libraries and in a 24/7 electronic universe.

We enhance Howard County's quality of life as a key partner in education, enriching culture, and strengthening community.

The Douglas County Libraries are a source of community pride and lifelong learning. Knowledgeable and friendly staff provide access to intellectual capital, showcase art and culture, and highlight local history through evolving collections and programs. Douglas County Libraries are good stewards of public funds

Worthington Libraries serve as community centers dedicated to lifelong learning, the exploration of new ideas and cultural exchange. As a vital part of the diverse community they serve, the libraries capitalize on opportunities to build innovative partnerships and aggressively promote services and programs. The libraries keep promises made to the community by exhibiting careful stewardship of resources and demonstrating fiscal responsibility through the collections and services provided.

The Cleveland Heights–University Heights Public Library is a community resource that nurtures the quest for lifelong learning, cultivates intellectual enrichment, promotes the enjoyment of reading, and opens the door to our children's imagination.

Figure 4.5. Sample Public Library Vision Statements

As Stewards of and guides to the record of human activity, we ensure and provide:

An environment of discovery and creativity

Successful use of the Library in learning, teaching and intellectual growth

Effective and integrated access to scholarly resources

Leadership in an emerging global network of libraries

An exemplary work environment where members participate, develop, and excel.

—Yale University

The Kelvin Smith Library is an integral component of a world-class university. Librarians work in partnership with members of the university to create and share knowledge, extend the boundaries of digital library research, and build an informed, civil community through:

Space designed for changing patterns of scholarship and learning as well as the changing lifestyles of faculty and students.

Access to rich and diverse research materials regardless of format, location or mode of access.

Transforming research and learning through the creation of digital libraries, electronic publishing services and open access awareness.

Personalized services tailored to individual needs and delivered whenever possible without regard for time and space constraints

Contributions to the local community that narrow Cleveland's digital opportunity gap.

Organizational effectiveness from evidence-based assessment, innovative marketing, coordinated planning and staff development that responds to strategic objectives.

—Case Western Reserve University

The University of Virginia Library facilitates research, teaching, and learning by providing:

easy access to superb collections, information, and services; and

physical places that welcome research, study, and discourse in an environment in which people and ideas are respected.

The Libraries: NC State's competitive advantage.

—North Carolina State University

Figure 4.6. Sample Academic Library Vision Statements

Writing a Vision Statement

The vision statement answers the question, "Where do we want to go?" in terms that describe a highly desirable future state for the community served by the library. Use the following template to create or update your library's vision statement:

We seek to become

_____

for (customers)

_____

USING A SLOGAN

Once a library has created its vision, it may want to create a slogan or tagline that summarizes that vision. This can be a handy way to refer to the library's vision in a form that will be short and memorable. The purpose of a slogan or tagline is to express the essence of the library's brand and its vision. The slogan can be very helpful for the library director and the management team as they try to convey the relevance and importance of the library's vision.

Examples of library slogans include the following:

- A World of Information
- Making Powerful Connections
- Answers NOW!
- Your Library Delivers
- Your Hub for Information and Ideas
- Be a Reader, Be Informed
- Delivering the World of Ideas to You
- Why go buy the book when you can go by the library?
- Read: Using your library is an investment in your future!

FACING THE OUTSIDE WORLD

Successful organizations in the nonprofit and governmental arenas have adopted 10 practices that have helped them achieve a preferred environment:

1. Center on mission.
2. Operate "just beyond the possible."
3. Embrace volatility.
4. Use the market as an ally.
5. Beware the source of funds.
6. Lower the barriers to external collaboration.

7. Harvest external support.

8. Prepare for hardball.

9. Pay attention to outcomes.

10. Change the prevailing wind.[8]

NOTES

1. David Osborne and Ted Gaebler, *Reinventing Government: How the Entrepreneurial Spirit is Transforming the Public Sector* (New York: Addison-Wesley, 1992).

2. Eileen Shapiro, *Fad Surfing in the Boardroom* (Reading, MA: Addison-Wesley, 1995), 15.

3. F. Drucker. *Managing the Non-Profit Organization* (New York: HarperBusiness, 1990), 5.

4. Linda K. Wallace, *Libraries, Mission, & Marketing: Writing Mission Statements That Work* (Chicago: American Library Association, 2004).

5. Gary Hamel and C. K. Prahalad, *Competing for the Future* (Boston: Harvard Business School Press, 1994). See also Gary Hamel, *Leading the Revolution* (Boston: Harvard Business School Press, 2000).

6. Steps to determine a mission statement's readability level:

   A. Compute the number of words.

   B. Compute the number of sentences.

   C. Compute the average number of words per sentence.

   D. Count the number of difficult words.

   E. Compute the number of difficult words per 100 words—a percentage.

   F. Compute the sum of the word average and the difficult word percentage—this is called the "Fog Index." A high Fog Index means the text is confusing!

   Adapted from Robert Gunning and Douglas Mueller, *How to Take the Fog Out of Writing* (Chicago: Dartnell Corporation, 1981).

7. For a discussion about competitors, see Michael Sullivan, "The Fragile Future of Public Libraries," *Public Libraries* 42, no. 5 (September/October 2003): 303–8.

8. Paul C. Light, *Sustaining Innovation: Creating Nonprofit and Government Organizations that Innovate Naturally* (San Francisco: Jossey Bass, 1998), 59.

5

Step 2: Strategy and Strategy Maps

People and their managers are working hard to be sure things are done right, that they hardly have time to decide if they are doing the right things.

—Stephen R. Covey[1]

In almost every case, the mission and vision statements developed by the library are too broad to guide day-to-day actions and resource allocation decisions. A library can make its mission and vision operational when it creates a strategy for how the vision will be achieved.[2]

Libraries create value by leveraging their tangible and intangible assets—highly skilled professional staff, the physical collection, providing access to electronic databases, the library's catalog and Web site, physical facilities for meetings and programs, and so forth. A library's strategy is the manner in which it intends to create value for its customers, stakeholders, and citizens. The formulation, execution, and measurement of strategy provide the basis to evaluate the strategy's effectiveness in order to ascertain whether adjustments need to be made. Strategy is *not* about continuing the past; it's about *creating the future*.

The balanced scorecard is a powerful management tool that facilitates the tracking of a library's actual performance compared to its planned objectives. The scorecard assists the library in identifying the measures that will reflect the library's strategy—how it expects to create sustainable value. It is suggested that the balanced scorecard have a maximum of three to four measures per perspective. This limit forces the library to identify and measure the truly critical variables that represent the library's strategy for value creation.

47

WHAT IS STRATEGY?

Think of strategy as a bridge: Values are the bedrock on which the piers of the bridge are planted, the near bank is today's reality, the far bank is the vision. Your strategy is the bridge itself.

—Gordon R. Sullivan[3]

Strategies are all about *how* the organization decides to organize its available resources to achieve its vision. If the library needs a bridge to cross a river, it has several options or strategies from which to choose. Such strategies might be to build a pontoon bridge, a suspension bridge, a truss bridge, and so forth; to outsource the building of the bridge; to move upstream and ford the river; and so forth.

Once the library has decided on one or two strategies to follow, it must not simply reside in a strategic planning document that is occasionally pulled from the shelf. Rather, all library staff members must be cognizant of the strategy as they go about their daily tasks.[4] An analysis of why some companies have failed to achieve their objectives, and the reason for the high turnover rate among CEOs, is that the companies had failed to execute their strategy, rather than that they chose a poor or wrong strategy.[5]

In short, strategy is a hypothesis about what drives an organization's success.

For many libraries, "strategy" is equivalent to a relatively long planning document that consists of lists of programs, tasks, and initiatives rather than the outcomes the library is attempting to achieve. Strategy must shift from what the library plans to *do* to what it intends to *accomplish,* and *how*.

As shown in Figure 5.1, a number of barriers may arise when implementing strategy. The barriers to successfully implementing the desired strategy for a library require concerted action to ensure that they are acknowledged and successfully breached.

- **The Vision Barrier.** Most organizations, including libraries, have a difficult time communicating their vision and strategies to their employees. Part of the problem is that the hierarchical organizational structure and climate result in the top management team assuming that the appropriate message gets passed down to all staff members. Making assumptions is dangerous, because they are often proven false.

- **The People Barrier.** Day-to-day problems and situations that need attending to mask or divert attention from the longer-term horizon of strategies. People need help focusing on the library's vision and strategies so that this does not happen.

- **The Resource Barrier.** A majority of organizations, and that includes libraries, do not link budgets to strategies. Rather, the budget process, despite the often lengthy and painful process of preparation, is in essence a matter of modifying last year's budget to meet the forecast or fiscal constraints. The preparation of the budget can afford the library the chance to carefully examine the priorities for the coming year and link these priorities to the strategic goals and objectives.

- **The Management Barrier.** Most regularly scheduled management meetings typically focus on two topics: responding to problems (putting out fires) and making sure that the library is staying within its budget. Little time is spent viewing the library from a broader perspective and ensuring that the day-to-day activities are aligned with meeting the library's vision and successfully implementing the planned strategies.

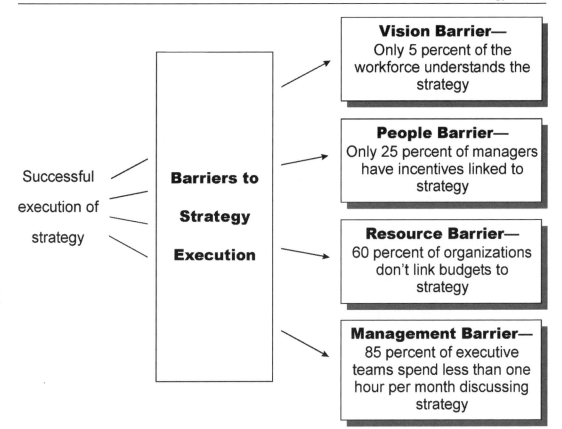

Successful execution of strategy → Barriers to Strategy Execution

Vision Barrier— Only 5 percent of the workforce understands the strategy

People Barrier— Only 25 percent of managers have incentives linked to strategy

Resource Barrier— 60 percent of organizations don't link budgets to strategy

Management Barrier— 85 percent of executive teams spend less than one hour per month discussing strategy

Figure 5.1. Barriers to Implementing Strategy. Adapted from material developed by Robert S. Kaplan and David P. Norton.

As Peter Senge has observed:

> Many leaders have personal visions that never get translated into shared visions that galvanize an organization. What has been lacking is a discipline for translating individual vision into shared vision.[6]

Larry Bossidy and Ram Charan have observed that strategic initiatives often fail due to resistance from managers who are waiting for the idea *du jour* to fail and so put little attention or effort into projects. They suggest that:

> The leader's personal involvement, understanding and commitment are necessary to overcome this passive (or in many cases active) resistance. She has not only to announce this initiative, but to define it clearly and define its importance to the organization. She can't do this unless she understands how it will work and what it really means in terms of benefit.[7]

The primary goal of any kind of strategic planning process is to identify the *results that matter*. Once the results that matter have been identified, the organization then must determine what major activities will enable it to achieve the desired results. This concept can be expressed as a formula:

$$R = f(a_1, a_2, a_3 \ldots)$$

Results that matter

Which activities will enable the library to achieve the results that matter?

Review/Adjust

Results/Measurement Focus

THREE BROAD STRATEGIES

There are three broad strategies that a library may wish to consider, as shown in Figure 5.2:[8]

- *Operational excellence* simply means that your library is the best at what it does. If you were a for-profit company, operational excellence would mean that you are the low-cost provider of particular products and services.

- Libraries interested in focusing on *customer intimacy* could develop "opt-in" programs whereby a customer provides additional personal information about reading or research preferences in exchange for more customized services from the library.

- Focusing on *innovative services* means more than simply adopting the use of the next "hot" technology. Although adopting the use of technology can be an asset for both the library as well as its customers, focusing on innovation means considering all of the services that the library provides or could provide, from the customer's perspective. Implementing innovation likely means that existing policies and procedures will need to be revised. After all, most management policies and processes are controlled by the defenders of the past.

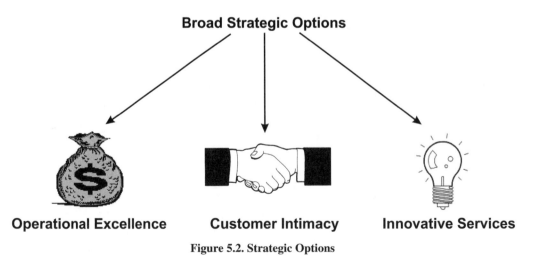

Broad Strategic Options

Operational Excellence   **Customer Intimacy**   **Innovative Services**

Figure 5.2. Strategic Options

Having a greater understanding of the needs of its customers and how it adds value will allow the library to make a better selection of what broad strategy to choose. To create superior value for the library's customers, it is necessary to have a clear understanding of what customers value and then translate their needs into specific products or services that will address those needs. The library could segment its community into three broad groups: frequent users, infrequent users, and nonusers. Frequent users could be further stratified into additional groups: children, teens, adults, seniors, and so forth. The library could conduct separate focus group meetings for each segment.

A library cannot choose to excel at all three strategic options. Rather, as a part of the planning process, it must decide to focus on one of the three options. Focus is not about efficiency in a cost sense; rather, it's about efficiency in a don't-get-distracted, get-all-the-energy moving in one direction sense. Ask yourself: What advantages would the library gain by being more narrowly focused?[9]

> *The main thing is to keep the main thing, the main thing.*
>
> —Jim Barksdale[10]

Remember that strategies are *not* the programmatic goals and objectives that most public libraries have historically developed on an annual basis. For example, some libraries develop programmatic goals that are grouped into several categories (services, technology, resources, and staff development). A strategy is a plan of action with a shared understanding designed to accomplish a specific goal.

If the library is medium to large in size and has branches, it may want to consider developing different kinds of branch facilities that provide a variety of services that will appeal to residents in the nearby neighborhood, as the Denver Public Library is doing.[11]

To identify and consider possible strategies to follow, the library should be able to answer the following questions:

- Why do customers choose to use the library (physically and electronically)?

- Why do some customers return repeatedly, whereas others don't come back after an initial visit?

- Why do some individuals never use the library—either physically or electronically?

- Who are the library's competitors? What advantages does the library have over its competitors?

- What weaknesses come to mind when considering the library and its services?

- What does the library want to be known for?

- How can the library add more value to its existing services?

- What new services should the library introduce?

- Are there one or more existing services that can be safely eliminated?

STEP 2A—CHOOSE TWO TO FOUR BROAD STRATEGIC THEMES

Your library should identify two to four broad organizational strategies or strategic themes that will distinguish the library from its competitors. The library's mission statement reflects what the library is currently providing. The vision statement articulates where the library would like to be at some point in the future (five or ten years from now). The resulting gap between now and the future becomes the focus for the library's planning activities.

Sometimes these broad strategic themes are called strategic objectives or goals. They should be a statement describing the important outcomes that are critical to achieving the library's vision. These outcomes should have the greatest impact on the library's customers. In other words, they should describe what the library must *achieve* to be successful in the future.

Strategic Themes

Strategic themes or objectives

- have a long-term results orientation;
- affect the entire library;
- are challenging, yet attainable within a realistic time frame;
- help distinguish the library from its competitors;
- do not reflect internal activities within the library;
- acknowledge the external forces that are shaping the library (and its competitors); and
- may require new funding, new services, and new staff (or existing staff may need to upgrade their skills).

These broad strategies should pervade the entire organizational culture. Once articulated, they should resonate with all staff members. Among these broad strategies might be the following:

- High levels of customer service
- Ready availability of physical resources
- Active and varied programming
- Responding to customer needs
- Stimulating learning
- Merchandizing of the library's collection
- Using technology to personalize service offerings
- Encouraging more customer self-help
- Providing an enriched library catalog
- Building and maintaining attractive facilities
- Providing amenities to foster social gatherings
- Responding with new services to meet changing demographics
- Customizing services to better meet the needs of a specific market segment

Many organizations, whether for-profit, nonprofit, or governmental, have difficulty deciding whom to serve and what services to provide and thus fall victim to the temptation of attempting to serve everyone with the broadest possible array of services. One of the real challenges of formulating a strategy is determining when to say no, when to pass on an opportunity that may arise, and what the library should focus on. When an organization attempts to be all things to all people, it usually does a very poor job at everything. Gary Hamel has noted that, "The essential problem in organizations today is a failure to distinguish *planning* from *strategizing*. In this context strategizing is critical to leading innovation."[12]

Identifying and articulating the strategies that are currently in place or deciding to pursue a new strategy has several benefits:

1. **Decision making can be improved.** Having a clearly articulated strategy allows an organization to view proposed initiatives and projects with a more clearly focused perspective, which t gives the management team and board a better basis for making decisions.

2. **Strategic thinking and action is promoted.** A strategy that is understood by everyone within an organization helps direct all staff members to make better decisions about how to spend their time and energies.

3. **Performance is enhanced.** A strategic focus within an organization will likely mean that the organization is energized and more likely to achieve its stated goals.[13] When all library staff members have a clear understanding of the library's strategies, day-to-day activities become much more focused.

Value-Impact Matrix

A useful tool that will assist the library in identifying priorities is a value-impact matrix, shown in Table 5.1 (page 54). The library should identify all of its current and planned services and activities, then place each service or activity in one of the four quadrants. Services that affect a large number of individuals (customers, for example) will have a high impact. Similarly, a service will have a value placed on it by the library's customers (high demand equals high value). Remember that the assessment of value and impact is from the customer's perspective, not the librarian's.

For the sample library shown in Table 5.1, the home-bound services, for example, will most likely affect very few members of the community and thus have a low value. Obviously your library will create a value-impact matrix that will have a different arrangement of library services than those shown in Table 5.1. Once the matrix has been created, the most important services will be identified and the library can begin to identify the strategies that will have the greatest effect on delivering high-value, high-impact services.

As noted in the discussion about strategies above, there are several ways in which the library can choose to deliver a particular service. For example, customer services in a public library may range from "wait till they ask at a service desk" to encouraging staff to wander around in the library in a more proactive manner (clearly identified by their clothing and/or name tag), observing body language as one indicator of the need for assistance. Similarly, once a customer asks for assistance, the staff member may "point to where a resource may be found" or use a more "hands-on" approach, accompanying the customer to ensure the resource is found and determining whether the customer needs additional assistance.

Table 5.1. Value-Impact Analysis

	Low Impact	High Impact
High Value	Programs Recruiting and training staff Local history collection Interlibrary loan—resource sharing Meeting rooms and study areas	Library collection—borrowing, using, and accessing materials Searching and downloading articles from online databases Summer reading program Computers for Internet access
Low Value	Reference service Bookmobile services Home-bound services Administrative services (HR, payroll, etc.)	Acquisitions, cataloging, and processing materials Facility maintenance and cleaning Equipment reliability

Deciding on the broad "philosophical" strategies that will identify the kind of public library you want to be will assist the library's scorecard team as they develop your library's scorecard. The broad strategies will allow the team to determine the more narrowly defined strategies and tactics that will move the library toward achieving its vision.

A simple technique for translating the broad top-level library strategies into the substrategies is called the "what/how" approach. Once the broad strategies have been determined, the discussion among the team members should move from "what is to be achieved" to "how this should be achieved."

For example, your library wants to have its collection used more intensively—the "what." The team may see several methods to achieve this—the "hows"—as shown in Figure 5.3. For each "how" option identified, the question "How many options are there to achieve this?" should also be asked.

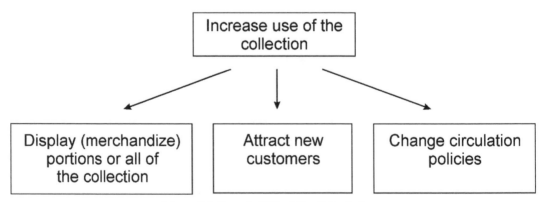

Figure 5.3. Sample "What/How" Technique

> *It is difficult to implement strategies if they can't be understood, and strategies can't be understood if they can't be described.*

STEP 2B—DECIDE ON THE STRUCTURE OF THE LIBRARY'S BALANCED SCORECARD

As noted in chapter 2, the library has the flexibility to design its own library scorecard in terms of what perspectives to include and the cause-and-effect relationships that exist between the perspectives. The scorecard team should thoroughly review and discuss a number of scorecard design options prior to making a final selection. Note that the library scorecard may well go through several iterations over g several weeks as people on the scorecard team become more familiar with the scorecard and its implications.

Once their review is finalized, the team should write up an explanation of their understanding of the cause-and-effect relationships among the perspectives. This explanation, along with a diagram of the library's balanced scorecard, should then be shown to other library staff members and library board members so that they can think about the scorecard and offer some feedback.

For purposes of illustration, the library balanced scorecard shown in Figure 5.4 (page 56) is used. Remember that your library should decide what perspectives should be included and in what order or sequence they should be arranged or organized, so that the resulting scorecard best reflects the circumstances and conditions in your own public library.

The process of identifying the specific components that are to be reflected in a library's strategy map starts at the top. In our illustration the "customer perspective" is at the top. Thus, the library asks the question: "To achieve our vision, how must we look to our customers?" What strategy is going to delight customers when they use the library (physically or electronically)? What must the library do to meet the needs of its customers? Typically organizations are concerned about market share, customer retention rate, and customer satisfaction. The balanced scorecard team should come up with a statement, sometimes called the strategic aim or core value, that encompasses the essence of the customer perspective. Examples of such a statement might be, "Having the right resources, right tools, and a helpful staff" or "We respond to the needs of our customers."

For the "information resources perspective" the question is: "To satisfy our customers, what information resources must we provide?" (access to the library's collection and electronic databases, programs, training, and so forth). What are the characteristics of the information resources that will best meet the needs of our customers? The answers to these questions are recognized in a statement about the information resources perspective. A potential statement might be, "A collection that focuses on meeting the current information needs of our community."

The "internal processes perspective" asks the question: "To satisfy our customers, what business process must we excel at?" Of particular importance for a library are those processes that are performed frequently and have an impact on the customer. Possible processes include circulation checkout, the time it takes an item to be returned to the shelf, cataloging and processing time, and so forth. Examples of such a statement might be, "Determine ways to significantly reduce wait times for services" or "We continuously improve our processes."

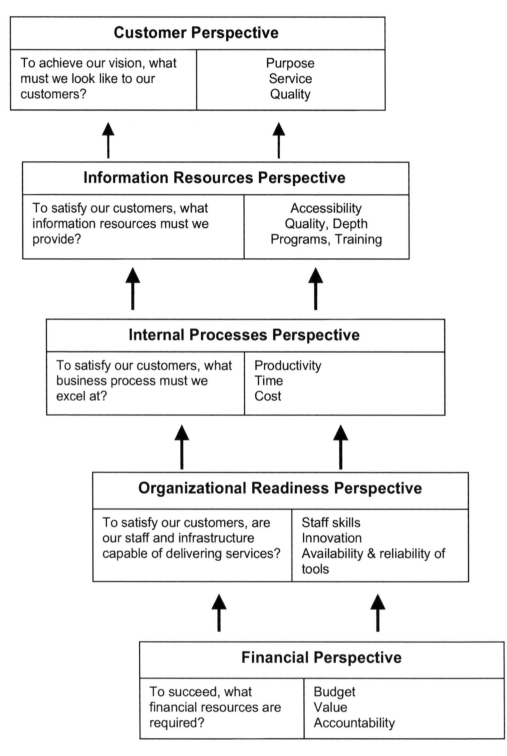

Figure 5.4. Illustrative Library Balanced Scorecard

The "organizational readiness perspective," in some cases called the "learning and growth perspective" focuses on the question: "To satisfy our customers, are our staff and infrastructure capable of delivering services?" One possible statement reflecting the strategic aim for this perspective might be, "Right people, right skills, right tools" or "We enable and develop our people and our systems."

The "financial perspective," sometimes called the "budget perspective," must ask the question: "To succeed, what financial resources are required?" Each year, the library's budget request must be reviewed and justified. The library must demonstrate that it is a good steward of the public's monies and that the community receives value for the funds entrusted to the library. A strategic aim for this perspective might be, "The library will have sufficient funding to provide the services the community expects" or alternatively, "We use our resources wisely."

The scorecard team should identify the strategic aim or core value for each perspective as shown in Figure 5.4 as the first step in creating its strategy map. The library will need to complete this form for each perspective. It is recommended that the team start at the top, which in our illustration is the customer perspective, and work its way down.

An example of how the library might complete this form is shown for the customer perspective:

Core Value: We respond to the needs of our customers.

Strategic Objectives:

- Retain existing customers

- Attract new customers

- Become the community's meeting place

STEP 2C—DEVELOP A STRATEGY MAP

The formulation of strategy is an art. The description of strategy, however, should not be an art. If we can describe strategy in a more disciplined way, we increase the likelihood of successful implementation. With a balanced scorecard that tells the story of the strategy, we now have a reliable foundation.

—Robert Kaplan and David Norton[14]

The balanced scorecard has evolved from providing a series of performance measures that described an organization's intangible assets into a powerful tool that can be used to describe, implement, and measure an organization's strategy. The scorecard is not a collection of performance measures in four or five independent perspectives but rather a series of cause-and-effect linkages of objectives among the perspectives selected by the library. These cause-and-effect linkages are called a *strategy map*.

Developing a strategy map is the real key to creating an effective balanced scorecard. You can think of a strategy map as the "secret ingredient" in a great BBQ sauce! The strategy map describes what the library needs to do to be successful. For some libraries, it may be better to utilize the current strategies the library is using as the basis for your library's strategy map, rather than embarking upon a strategic planning process.[15] The scorecard provides a framework for a library to move from selecting a strategy to doing it.

The use of a strategy map can assist the library in communicating its vision to all staff and members of the community. The map is intended to help the management team explain the library's strategy. Remember that it takes time—and repetition—for people to absorb it.

Robert Kaplan and David Norton have developed a general purpose strategy map (see Figure 5.5). This general purpose strategy map can be used to identify the likely strategies within each perspective that might be considered by the library as it develops its own strategy map. The map is a visual tool to assist the library in describing its strategy so that measures and their associated targets that are related to strategy can be selected.

It would be helpful for the scorecard team to carefully study the strategy map shown in Figure 5.5. This figure illustrates the most likely strategic objectives that can be chosen by the library.

The library should limit the number of strategic objectives to no more than three or four. The idea is to identify the most important strategic objectives rather than attempting to develop an exhaustive list. One of the by-products of developing a library balanced scorecard is to assist the library in concentrating on a small but significant set of objectives. The "shotgun" or "let's do everything" approach inevitably leads to mediocre services.

The strategy map provides a visual framework for a library's strategy—how it intends to create value for its customers. A good strategy map will link together

- the overall customer value proposition,

- the desired productivity goals for internal processes,

- the capabilities required from the library itself (staff skills, information technology ,and leadership),

- the characteristics of a physical collection and electronic database access provision, and

- the budget and other financial resources required to deliver the library's vision.

After the scorecard team has worked through the strategy options shown in Figure 5.5, it should prepare a graphic version of its strategy map. The team might want to use the strategy map template shown in Figure 5.6 (page 60). Each strategic objective is placed in a "bubble" within the appropriate perspective.

Some organizations, especially in the for-profit sector, are able to establish clear cause-and-effect relationships between strategic objectives linking the perspectives. These links are typically shown as arrows in most strategy maps. Such arrows are not necessary, although desirable, in the public library setting.

It is important to recognize that the lower portions of the strategy map are the "drivers" that enable the library to fulfill the strategic objectives found in the higher perspectives. The goal is to creatively link the objectives in each of the perspectives that allows the library to gain insights into how it can better serve its community as well as communicating a captivating story of the library and its accomplishments.

The process of creating a strategy map for a library is summarized in Figure 5.7 (page 61).

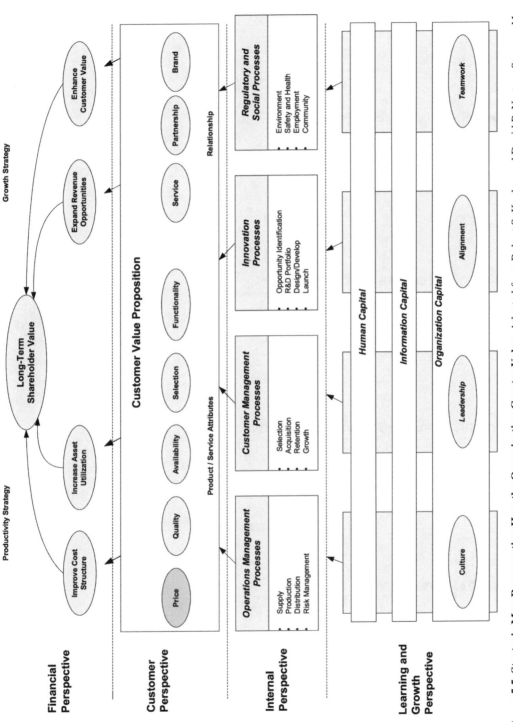

Figure 5.5. Strategic Map Representing How the Organization Creates Value. Adapted from Robert S. Kaplan and David P. Norton, *Strategy Maps: Converting Intangible Assets into Tangible Outcomes* (Boston: Harvard Business School Press, 2004), 331.

59

Customer Perspective

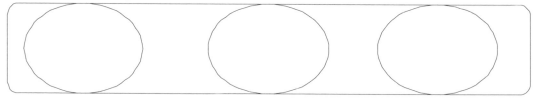

Information Resources Perspective

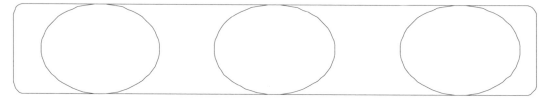

Internal Processes Perspective

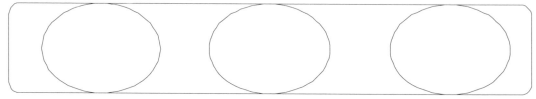

Organizational Readiness Perspective

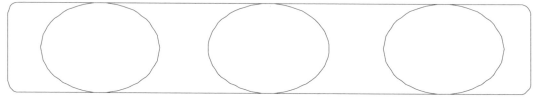

Financial Perspective

Figure 5.6. Library Strategy Map Template

60

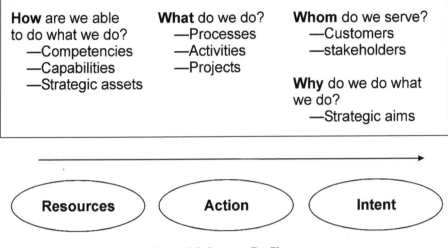

Figure 5.7. Strategy Profile

SMART MANAGERS

Smart managers go beyond the preparation of a mission statement and a vision statement in a number of significant ways. What these managers do differently is

- state their strategies publicly;

- communicate their strategies to every staff member, every time an opportunity presents itself;

- believe passionately in their strategies;

- acknowledge that the implementation of their strategies is dependent on all staff members;

- hold all staff members, especially management, accountable; and

- systematically measure the progress the organization is making in achieving its vision.

NOTES

1. Stephen R. Covey, *The Seven Habits of Highly Effective People: Restoring the Character Ethic* (New York: Simon & Schuster, 1989), 74.

2. Robert S. Kaplan and David P. Norton. "How Strategy Maps Frame an Organization's Objectives," *Financial Executive* (March/April 2004): 40–45.

3. Quoted in William A. Schiemann and John H. Lingle. *Bullseye! Hitting Your Strategic Targets Through High-Impact Measurement* (New York: Free Press, 1999), 61.

4. Michel Porter. "What Is Strategy?" *Harvard Business Review* (November/December 1996): 61–79.

5. R. Charan and G. Colvin, "Why CEOs Fail," *Fortune* 139 (June 21, 1999): 68–78. A similar analysis performed in the 1980s noted the same result. See Walter Kiechel, "Corporate Strategies Under Fire," *Fortune* 106 (December 27, 1982): 34–39.

6. Peter Senge, *The Fifth Discipline* (New York: Currency, 1994), 64.

7. Larry Bossidy and Ram Charan, *Execution* (New York: Crown Business, 2002), 65.

8. Michael Treacy and Fred Wiersema, *The Discipline of Market Leaders: Choose Your Customers, Narrow Your Focus, Dominate Your Market* (New York: Addison-Wesley, 1995).

9. Gary Hamel, *Leading the Revolution* (Boston: Harvard Business School Press, 2000).

10. Jim Barksdale, quoted in George Labovitz and Victor Rosansky, *The Power of Alignment: How Great Companies Stay Centered and Accomplish Extraordinary Things* (New York: Wiley, 1997), 1.

11. Denver Public Library, "Wake Up Call: What Our Customers Are Trying to Tell Us . . . If We'd Only Listen" (Presentation at the Public Library Conference, March 2006, Boston, Massachusetts).

12. Gary Hamel, "Strategy as Revolution," *Harvard Business Review* 74 (July/August 1996), 71.

13. For a more detailed discussion of strategic planning, see Joseph R. Matthews, *Strategic Planning and Management for Library Managers* (Westport, CT: Libraries Unlimited, 2005).

14. Robert S. Kaplan and David P. Norton, *The Strategy-Focused Organization* (Boston: Harvard Business School Press, 2001).

15. See Robert S. Kaplan and David P. Norton, *Strategy Maps: Converting Intangible Assets into Tangible Outcomes* (Boston: Harvard Business School Press, 2004). See also Paul R. Niven, *Balanced Scorecard Step-by-Step for Government and Nonprofit Agencies* (New York: Wiley, 2004).

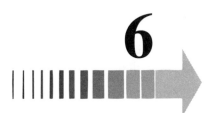

Step 3: Selecting Performance Measures

Historically, libraries have embraced a variety of performance measures,[1] illustrated in Figure 6.1. Originally libraries used input measures both as a means to compare a library with other similar libraries and to communicate with their funding decision makers. During the 1980s, libraries moved to embrace output measures, and more recently, at the urging of the Institute of Museums and Library Services, are attempting to develop outcome measures of library services.[2]

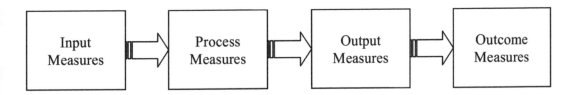

Figure 6.1. Evaluation Model

INPUT MEASURES

Input measures identify the resources provided to the library. While most libraries use fiscal input measures, such measures may also include staff, materials, equipment and space. These measures identify the total costs of operating the library as well as the mix of resources used to provide all of the library's services.

PROCESS MEASURES

> *Measures of productivity do not lead to improvement in productivity.*
>
> —W. Edwards Deming[3]

Process measures focus on the activities, processes, or procedures used to transform the resources into services provided by the library. Often process measures are called "productivity measures" and quantify the time, costs, or quality (accuracy) of a particular task or activity.

Process or efficiency measures relate "outputs" to "inputs." Such measures are often expressed in terms of cost per transaction (activity) or time per activity. Process measures are designed to answer the question, Are we doing *things* right?

Usually a library will measure itself against other "comparable" libraries to determine whether it is performing various activities in a cost effective manner. The focus on process improvements within a library should be on the organization's ability to deliver improved or new services that are valued by the library's customers.

OUTPUT MEASURES

These descriptive measures are counts of the use of library services and reflect volume of activity. Such measures have been used to reflect the "goodness" of the library, because the library is being heavily used. Measures may reflect use of library services, the library's physical collection, use of electronic databases and the library's Web site, as well as the quality of services. The focus of output measures is the library itself.

OUTCOME MEASURES

Outcome measures focus on the impact the library has in the lives of its customers in the short term and ultimately upon the community as a whole. The Institute of Museums and Library Services has defined outcomes as changes in attitude, skill, knowledge, behavior, status, or condition. Some individuals have suggested that it is possible to divide outcomes into personal/social benefits and economic benefits. Others have suggested that there are three types of outcomes: immediate, intermediate, and long term.

Joan Durrance and Karen Fisher have suggested that the library's central outcome is access to reading materials. They posit that some outcome measures have an inward focus and include sustaining a sense of identity, life enrichment, and added emotional support. Outcome measures with an outward application include social connections and connections to the larger world.[4] In most cases it is easier to develop outcome measures for a specific library service than for all library services.

The key to developing useful outcome measures is constructing a clear logic model. A *logic model* establishes the links among a library's services or activities, the results these activities produce, and how the results will be measured. That is, **if** the library provides a particular service, **then** there are a series of related changes or benefits for the library's customer. For example, **if** the library provides a homework assistance program (purchases copies of materials suggested by teachers, staff, and volunteer tutors and provides a place to work with tutors), **then** the children will complete their homework assignments, undergo a more positive learning experience, and achieve better grades than their peers who do not participate in the library's homework program.

Because information about the ultimate result or impact of the library is not always available or practicable to measure, proxy or surrogate measures are sometimes used. Outcome measures are only indirectly about the library—their real focus is the impact of the library on its customers. Rhea Rubin has developed a series of steps a library can follow to make outcomes measurable.[5]

Congress passed the Government Performance and Results Act (GPRA) in 1993 requiring federal agencies to report the outcomes of their services and activities. The Institute of Museums and Library Services (IMLS) has embraced outcome-based evaluation, and over the next few years state library agencies and library grant recipients will be required to demonstrate the use of outcome-based performance measures.

Customer satisfaction . . . is neither outcome nor output. Rather, it is a qualitative assessment of library outputs.

—Jennifer Cram[6]

Avoid the temptation to treat performance measures as an end, rather than as a means. Combining the input, process, output, and outcome measures from the evaluation model with each perspective, as shown in Table 6.1, illustrates the reality that some types of measures are more suitable for some perspectives than others.

Table 6.1. Possible Performance Measures for Each Perspective

Perspectives	Inputs	Process	Outputs	Outcomes
Customer				✓
Information Resources	✓	✓	✓	
Internal Processes		✓		
Organizational Readiness	✓	✓	✓	
Financial	✓			

The vast majority of performance measures historically used by libraries are internally focused. That is, the input, process, and output measures reflect what the library receives and converts into services that are used by its community. The challenge is to balance this internal focus through the use of some measures that reflect the impact of the library on the lives of individuals and the community at large.

Nothing is good or bad but by comparison.

—Thomas Fuller[7]

Use of number of staff (FTE) in a performance measure is problematic because it does not acknowledge possible changes over time or differences between libraries in

- staff skills and abilities,
- costs (pay rates plus fringe benefits),
- amount of overtime worked,
- actual work time during a week,
- a large part-time staff versus a smaller full-time staff, and
- The possibility of outsourcing some tasks or activities.

Performance measures can be derived using a number of different methods, including, among others,

- a count of transactions (manually or automatically),
- a calculation using data stored in an automated system,
- a survey of a sample of the population (using a printed instrument, the Internet, or by telephone), and
- an assessment by a trained individual—including a mystery shopper.

Performance measures provide an ongoing mechanism for measuring the library's success in channeling its resources toward achieving its vision. Having a vision that is measurable will allow the library to answer the question, How will we know when we get there?

A strategy without measures is just a wish, and measures that are not aligned with strategy are a waste of time.

STEP 3A—CREATE A LIST OF POSSIBLE MEASURES

Each member of the scorecard team should independently develop a list of possible performance measures for each strategic objective within each perspective. When the team meets, the members should share their measures and create a long list of possible measures for each objective for each perspective. A discussion of each of the proposed measures should take place, as well as the possibility of developing as yet unidentified measures or combining two or more measures. D. Simply collect all of the suggestions. Determining the utility of each suggestion will occur in a later step.

Depending on the library's perspective and the focus of the measurement activity, performance measures can reflect an organizational process or individual activities, as shown in Table 6.2.

Table 6.3 (page 68–69) is a "shopping list" of measures that might be developed by your library. Your list of measures should, and will, differ according to the strategies chosen by your library.

> **Tip!** Try not to be constrained by "traditional" library measures, but rather identify measures that will reflect the library's progress in achieving its vision.

There is a tendency among libraries to consider only the measures that are currently being collected or that would be easy to collect. The library may also want to select a measure that will make it "look good." These tendencies need to be resisted. The library should focus on identifying what measures will reflect the strategic objectives identified when the library created its strategy map.

Table 6.2. Three Levels of Performance Measures

Level/Outcomes	Objectives	Design	Measurement Perspective
Organization	Overarching strategy	Strategy-driven functions	Customer perspective
	The customer value proposition	Cost-benefit analysis	Information
	Organizational alignment	Understanding costs of activities	Resources perspective
	The business plan		Internal processes perspective
			Organizational readiness perspective
			Financial perspective
Process	Conformance to customer standards	Inputs	Cost
		Outputs	Cycle time
		Process owner	Quality
		Boundary spanning	Quantity
Job	Report cards	Process maps	Outcomes
	Motivation	Function charts	Target measures
	Selection	Task analysis	Activities

Table 6.3. Possible Performance Measures

City-Provided Funds	**Non-City Funding**
$/capita	Percent of budget from nongovernment sources
Total funding $	Nongovernment $/capita
Growth in budget after inflation	Total funding $
Budget/borrower	Funding/borrower
Budget/cardholder	Number of funders
Budget as a percent of government budget	Value of volunteer hours
Nonpersonnel budget	Grants applied for and received
Maximize asset utilization	
Identify/Launch Innovations	**Best Practices**
Number of innovations implemented	Number of changes in procedures/year
Total number of staff hours	Number of BP topics researched
Number of innovation opportunities	Comparative statistics
Budget for innovation	Services library does not offer
Research grants received	Unique services library offers
Internal Communications	**Hiring and Promoting Staff**
Staff survey	Staff morale survey
Staff ratings of internal service activities (administration, IT, HR, payroll, maintenance, etc.)	Absenteeism rate
	Staff turnover
	Average number of qualified applicants/opening
	Percent of MLS staff
	Compensation compared to other libraries
	Number of jobs filled—internal versus external
	Budget for staff recognition
Staff Competencies	**Reliable IT**
Assessment survey	Network reliability (percent)
Training hours/staff member	Average age of all computers
Number of workshops offered to staff	IT budget
Number of workshops attended/staff member	Number of IT staff hours/week
Number of mentoring opportunities	Time to fix a hardware component
Training budget	Number of records with problems due to ILS
Travel and meeting budget	Number of aides and systems staff/number of computers
Percent of staff who complete career development plan	ILS system reliability
	Availability and reliability of tools
Collection	**Electronic Resources**
Acquisitions budget percent/Total $	Electronic resources budget precent/total $
Acquisitions $/capita	Number of articles downloaded/year
Percent use/percent collection	Number of unique users (number/percent local residents)
In-library use/capita	Electronic resources: number of articles downloaded/year
Collection size/capita	
Collection turnover rate	Number of databases available
Availability survey	Number of sessions (in-library and remote)
Number of items with lost status	Total session time
Collection profile/population profile	
Library Web site	**Programming**
Number of times accessed/year	Total number of programs
Number of documents downloaded	Total attendance at programs
Usability of site	Program evaluation
Number of broken links	New experiences initiated
Time to load the first page	Testimonials
Number of links to Web site from other sites	
Usability testing of library Web site	

Operational Excellence	Overall Productivity
Time to reshelve items	Circulation $/circulated item
Time from order to on shelf	T.S. $/item added to collection
Reference quality	Reference budget/query
Reshelving accuracy rate	Circulation/clerk hour
Number of complaints/praise reports (letters, e-mails, and phone calls)	Circulation/staff member
	Number of items added/T.S. staff hour
Wait time for a hold	Number of reference queries/staff hour
Circulation queue wait times	Number of process improvements/year
	Circulation $/staff member
	Circulation $/hour open

Availability	Selection
Collection availability survey	Circulation percent compared to holdings percent
Total hours open/year	ILL requests—down
Number of people in queue to use a computer	Age of collection (percent added in last 4 years)
Average wait time to use a computer	Number of titles on hold
Wait time for items on hold	Average number of copies of best sellers
Evening hours compared to nearby library	Copies to hold ratio
Weekend hours compared to nearby library	Number of new titles added/year
ILL ratio	Topic or subject
Number of hold items not picked up	
Percent of titles added annually as a percent of total collection	
New titles added in last 5 years as a percent of total collection	
Materials turnover rate	
Percent circ compared to percent of holdings	
Percent of all new materials circulated in first 2 years	

Customer	Brand
Customer satisfaction survey	Marketing budget as a percent of total
Mystery shopper ratings	Brand recognition by public
Number of complaints/praises	
Satisfaction/customer segments	
Number of complaints/praise (letters, e-mails, and phone calls)	

Overall Value	
Cost-benefit analysis	
Total use (gate count + Web site visits)	
Total budget/total use	
Percent residents with library card	
Percent of total use by local residents	
Percent of registered borrowers who are local residents	
Percent cardholders who used library in last year	
Percent nonresidents as a percent of total card holders	
Number of programs and attendees	
Number/percent of cardholders who obtained library card and never returned	
Gate count	
Economic impact survey (nonresidents)	
Telephone survey of information needs	

One accurate measurement is worth more than 1,000 expert opinions.

—Grace Hooper[8]

Each of the data collection techniques has strengths and weaknesses. You will find the following:

- Focus groups, customer panels, and individual interviews are most important to answer the question, What service characteristics matter most to your customers?

- Surveys are most helpful to answer, How well are we doing relative to customer expectations and our competitors?

- Suggestion and complaint forms tell you what's wrong or missing. The average happy customer will tell three other people about his or her experience, whereas the unhappy customer will tell up to nine people.[9]

- Mystery shoppers provide a fairly accurate assessment of various library services and your facilities.

STEP 3B—SELECT YOUR FINAL MEASURES

Perhaps *the* most important factor for success in using the balanced scorecard is ensuring that you are measuring the right things. Given the truism that "what gets measured gets managed," measuring the wrong things will devote time, attention, and energy to activities that do not contribute to the success of the library.

In any number of areas of life the 80/20 rule, sometimes called the Pareto Principle, will apply. In this case, 20 percent of the potential measures will likely give you 80 percent of the information you need!

For a variety of reasons, most libraries collect a plethora of performance measures but do not understand the relationships between the measures. The management team should identify and focus on measures that will make a difference. It is crucial to understand that "leading" performance measures, such as quality and timeliness of a process, will affect the "lagging" indicators—customer satisfaction, increasing market share, and so forth.

From the list of possible measures, the scorecard team should make a final selection of measures. Remember that the goal is to select three to five measures per perspective.

Among the criteria a library might employ to make its final selection of performance measures are the following:

- **Strategic.** The measures assess the strategies that have been selected by the library.

- **Customer focused.** The measures reflect the views of customers and other stakeholders.

- **Timely.** The measures use current data that reflect existing conditions.

- **Accurate.** The data are not open to bias, interpretation, or inaccuracies.

- **Meaningful.** The measures are significant and relate to the library's vision and choice of strategies.

- **Understandable.** The measures can be easily explained and understood.

- **Balanced.** The measures include several types, that is, input, process, output, and outcomes.

- **Comparable.** The measures are useful for making comparisons over time with other "peer" libraries.

- **Impact.** The measures show the impact of the strategies and actions over time. They identify trends, comparisons to a baseline, etc.

- **Cost effective.** Data collection efforts are not expensive.

- **Simple.** The measures are relatively easy to calculate, interpret, and understand.

- **Cautious of averages.** Averages often conceal more than they reveal, so the measures should portray a true picture. For example, the number of customers who are extremely satisfied is more important than the average rating.[10]

- **Directed.** The selected measures must drive the right kind of behavior. People act on and respond to what gets measured.

Libraries should recognize that the use of performance measures is a means to an end and not the ultimate destination. The choice of performance measures should be SMART:

- **Specific:** accurate

- **Measurable:** quantifiable

- **Action oriented:** reflect critical processes

- **Relevant:** vital or important

- **Timely:** do not require a significant amount of time to gather and analyze the data[11]

Some measures may be collected on an annual basis, for example, customer satisfaction, whereas other measures are collected more frequently. The more important measures a library may consider are shown in Table 6.4.

Table 6.4 Possible Performance Measures

Collections	Routine Tasks	Service
Accessibility	Accuracy	Helpful
Currency	Timeliness	Informed
Depth and breath of coverage		Friendly
Availability		Professional

Source of Data

It is also important to consider the impact of data collection efforts on library staff members. In declining order of preference, the library should

- use existing data for a measure;

- analyze existing computer data (reports from the library's automated system);

- use sampling to gather the data rather than attempting to record every activity or transaction;

- use Web-based surveys or a touch-screen device to collection survey data, so that the data can be easily downloaded into a spreadsheet for further analysis;[12] and

- minimize any manual data collection efforts. The less intrusion into the daily activities of library staff members, the better.

Creative Measures

It is vital that the library select measures that will reflect how well a particular strategy is doing. Although some more "traditional" performance measures can be used, your library should also choose some new and nontraditional measures, such as

- asset utilization, which compares theoretical capacity with actual use (meeting rooms, equipment);

- freshness of the library's collection;

- tracking the movement of the audiovisual collection to disc-only format;

- use of a mystery shopper to rate facilities and staff performance;

- asking customers to identify the priority or importance of library services prior to asking them to rate actual performance;

- a collection relevance measure, which compares percent usage to percent of holdings;

- determining computer application availability of each desktop;

- a share-of-the-pie budget allocation from a government entity; and

- improved test scores by literacy participants.

STEP 3C—COMPLETE A PERFORMANCE MEASURE RECORD SHEET

Once the final measures have been selected, the team should divide up responsibility for the measures among the team members. A team member should identify the current value for each measure (assuming the value can be immediately determined). The value for each measure will be needed for the next step, when targets are selected for each measure.

One of the challenges facing any library is that its automated system does not provide the flexibility for a library to create a new measure. For example, consider the need to identify all individuals who have used the library in some way in the past year (to determine what percent of all potential customers are using the library). The automated system will identify those individuals who have borrowed material but cannot also identify those who have logged onto the library's Web site to search an electronic resource or have attended a library program (but did not borrow materials). Well, you get the idea. It's a challenge.

Tip! Software is available that will assist the library in storing, analyzing, and presenting performance measures for the balanced scorecard. The cost of such software ranges from several hundred dollars to more than $100,000!

It is *not* recommended that a library consider automating this process until it has produced four or more scorecards. Storing the data in a spreadsheet is one handy way to keep track of the information and assist in producing graphs and charts. Manipulating the data by hand will force the scorecard team to carefully and systematically review the accuracy and value of each measure. Every scorecard will, inevitably, require some adjustments over time.

Software selection criteria might include such factors as visualization of performance results, number of perspectives that can be included, the database used to store data, compatibility with existing information technology architecture, technical support, and ease of use.

NOTES

1. See, for example, Peggy D. Rudd, "Documenting the Difference: Demonstrating the Value of Libraries Through Outcome Measurement," in *Perspectives on Outcome Based Evaluation for Libraries and Museums* (Washington, DC: Institute of Museum and Library Services, 2000). Available at http://www.imls.gov/pubs/pdf/pubobe.pdf.

2. Quoted in Will Kaydos, *Operational Performance Measurement: Increasing Total Productivity* (New York: St. Lucie Press, 1999), 29.

3. W. Edwards Deming, *Out of the Crisis* (Cambridge, MA: MIT Press, 1986), 64.

4. Joan C. Durrance and Karen E. Fisher, *How Libraries and Librarians Help: A Guide to Identifying User-Centered Outcomes* (Chicago: American Library Association, 2005), 161–64.

5. Rhea Joyce Rubin, *Demonstrating Results: Using Outcome Measurement in Your Library* (Chicago: American Library Association, 2006).

6. "Six Impossible Things Before Breakfast: A Multidimensional Approach to Measuring the Value of Libraries," in *Proceedings of the 3rd Northumbria International Conference on Performance Measurement in Libraries and Information Services: Newcastle upon Tyne, Information North, 2000*, 19–29.

7. Quoted in Kaydos, *Operational Performance Measurement*, 15.

8. Quote in Rocky J. Dwyer, "Utilizing Points of Differentiation to Enhance Competitiveness and Growth: Some Thoughts for Consideration," *Performance Measurement and Metrics* 5, no. 2 (2004): 66–71.

9. The Technical Assistance Research Programs Institute is located in Washington, D.C.

10. Frederick F. Reichheld, "The One Number You Need to Grow," *Harvard Business Review* 81, no. 12 (December 2003): 46–54.

11. J. L. Harbour, *The Basics of Performance Measurement* (Portland, OR: Productivity Press, 1997).

12. For a Web-based customer satisfaction survey, consider using the LibQUAL+ instrument, which can be licensed from the Association of Research Libraries. ARL can be contacted at (202) 296-2296 or www.arl.org/stats. A sample LibQUAL+ report is available at http://www.libqual.org/documents/SampleLibQUALNotebook.pdf.

7

Step 4: Identifying Targets and Initiatives

IDENTIFYING TARGETS

The library balanced scorecard facilitates measuring actual performance and reporting results compared to expectations or targets for each measure. Targets are used to answer the question, "What level for each measure must the library achieve to be successful?" Any variation becomes a focus for analysis. Remedial actions can be studied and a course of action can be implemented. In most cases, targets should require an improvement to existing processes and activities.

Long-term and intermediate targets can be determined so that library staff members can celebrate success when the intermediate target is reached and not become discouraged when the library does not achieve its goals quickly.

STEP 4A—ESTABLISH BASELINE PERFORMANCE

The library's scorecard team should determine the existing or baseline data for each measure. Note that the data for some measures may only be collected annually, so the existing baseline will not be known for some time. Alternatively, the library may use the data from the prior year. Establishing the baseline point for each measure answers the question, Where are we now? Establishing a baseline allows the library to monitor progress and improvement.

The library's scorecard team may want to divide up the gathering of baseline data for each of the performance measures.

STEP 4B—ESTABLISH TARGETS FOR EACH MEASURE

The importance of establishing targets cannot be overstated. A review of numerous studies found that performance improves by an average of 16 percent in organizations that establish targets.[1]

The challenge in establishing targets is that they must simultaneously be attainable and yet remain targets. A target is a quantifiable result expected within a specified period of time. If they are set too low, the targets will be achieved with little or no effort. If they are set too high, staff will likely become frustrated at their lack of progress. The tendency for most organizations is to set targets too low.

The library may want to determine what comparable libraries are currently achieving in each measure. This would help establish a range of data values for the performance measure. Library staff could chat with their peers in the profession and find out which libraries are doing a particularly good job in a particular area. The library might also determine what benchmarking reports exist, both within and outside the library field, which can be reviewed to help establish targets.

The process of setting performance targets to create challenging but achievable targets is an art. It is helpful to have a clear understanding of the range of potential values for a particular measure by reviewing comparable libraries.

When setting targets, a number of options are available:

- **Slam-dunk targets.** Such targets have already been achieved but are hidden, to the extent that others are not aware of the current performance. By this means, maintaining the status quo can be represented as an improvement.

- **Cakewalk targets.** Such targets seek to keep improvement very much in reach; a "little bit more" is good enough.

- **Reachable targets.** Such targets represent a goal that is reachable with concerted effort. Many organizations establish a target that is a 60 to 80 percent improvement over a three- to four-year time period, if no other rationale can be used to establish a target.

- **Stretch targets.** These targets are sometimes called "Big, Hairy Audacious Goals" or BHAG! For example, the library might decide to set a stretch target for the time it takes to return items to the shelf after they are returned. The Singapore Public Library established a goal in 2000 to have returned items back on the shelf within 15 minutes of their return. By 2006, items were back on the shelf within an average of 7 minutes.[2]

  Stretch targets are required when organizations embark on a Six Sigma quality improvement program. Six Sigma establishes a target that is six standard deviations from the mean, or a product or service quality rate of 99.99985% (1.5 defects per million). This clearly is a true stretch target, and yet a number of companies around the world have achieved such targets within a period of three to five years.[3]

It is not surprising that many organizations rely on using the "scientific wild ass guess," or SWAG, approach to establishing targets until such time as the organization has more experience about what is possible. Make sure to involve staff in considering the selection of targets for each measure. Their participation and input is important. As the library gains experience in using its balanced scorecard, it is not unusual for the library to adjust the targets in some manner.

Knowing the score is not the objective—changing it is.

—C. J. McNair[4]

STEP 4C—IDENTIFY INITIATIVES

It is more than likely that your library will identify and implement a number of projects or initiatives to reach one or more targets. These initiatives will likely require staff members to identify new ways of performing work as well as gathering new performance measures. The purpose of these initiatives is to assist the library in reaching its goals, as measured by reaching the targets identified for each measure included in the library's balanced scorecard.

It may not be necessary to identify an initiative in order for the library to meet or exceed a specific target.

Rather than attempting to develop a lengthy list of initiatives, much better results will be achieved if the initiatives are prioritized in terms of what will improve the library's ability to deliver on its strategies. Part of the priority setting process should be to identify the following for each initiative:

- A sponsor

- An implementation schedule

- What resources will be required

- Budgetary implications

It may be necessary for the library to improve on its processes in order to achieve some of its targets. There are several approaches to making improvements in the tasks or activities performed by the library. Look for ways to

- eliminate it,

- simplify it, and

- automate it.

STEP 4D—PRIORITIZE INITIATIVES

Aim to improve the things that will make a real difference—significant customer value, those with large costs, those with substantial consequences, etc.

Once the library has developed a list of initiatives that it can undertake, it should prioritize them using two principal criteria:

- What are the associated costs and benefits, or outcomes, for each initiative? Some initiatives or projects will be limited in scope and require few resources and may or may not have a significant impact. Other initiatives may be large and require considerable resources (budget and staff time) and may or may not have sizable returns.

- Will the initiative assist the library in moving toward its strategic objectives and ultimately in moving closer to its vision of the future? Initiatives that do not move the library ahead in reaching its vision should be discarded or assigned a very low priority.

The most desirable initiatives are those that will affect several of the library's objectives simultaneously.

Once the list of initiatives have been finalized, it is important for the library to implement the initiatives in a logical manner rather than attempting to start all of the projects simultaneously. The library should create an action plan for each initiative that will track what resources are necessary to accomplish ite, who is responsible for it, and the planned completion date. The library can then use these action plans to track the progress of implementing each initiative over the coming months.

One potential problem to avoid is attempting to complete too many initiatives simultaneously. (Taking too big a "bite" will likely lead to digestion problems!) It is always a good idea to identify an initiative that will lead to an "early win" that all staff members will recognize and celebrate. It is also important to create a timeline for all of the initiatives, because one or more projects may require that another initiative be completed before they can commence.

An overview of the balanced scorecard process is provided in Figure 7.1, which illustrates the role of initiatives in the overall process. Your library may want to replicate this figure using Excel so that each of the measures can be more easily updated on a quarterly basis.

The success of initiatives should be based on data, not opinions.

NOTES

1. Edwin A. Locke, "Motivation by Goal Setting," in *Handbook of Organizational Behavior,* ed. R. T. Golembiewski, 43–56 (New York: Marcel Dekker, 2001).

2. Roger Hallowell, Carin-Isabel Knoop, and Neo Boon Siong, *Transforming Singapore's Public Libraries.* Case Study 9-802-009 (Boston: Harvard Business School, October 2001).

3. Locke, "Motivation by Goal Setting," 43–56.

4. C. J. McNair, quoted in Mohan Nair, *Essentials of Balanced Scorecard* (New York: Wiley, 2004), 180.

Strategy Map		Balanced Scorecard		Action Plan	
Strategic Theme	Objectives	Measurement	Target	Initiative	Budget
Customer Perspectives	Increase customer satisfaction	Customer satisfaction survey	98 percent	Marketing campaign	$ XXX
Customer Satisfaction	Reduce customer complaints	Number of complaints	Reduce by 40 percent	Conduct annual focus groups	$ XXX
Information Resources Perspective	Materials selection aligned with demand	% circ compared to % holdings	Less than a 5 percent difference	Conduct a materials survey availability survey	$ XXX
Meet Demand / Right Collection	More copies for high demand titles	Decrease hold wait times to 2 weeks	Decrease by 40 percent	Update collection selection policies	$ XXX
Internal Perspective	Improve service delivery time	Cat. & processing times	7 days for all materials	Prepare a work flow analysis	$ XXX
Productivity improvements	Reduce queuing times	Checkout wait times	Less than 3 minutes	Consider outsourcing processing	$ XXX
Organizational Readiness Perspective	Increase staff training	# staff training hours/year	Increase to 40 hours / year	Formalize consistent training	$ XXX
Skilled Staff	More flexibility in automated library system	Automated system vendor response to enhancement requests	75 percent included in next release	Invite vendor to library for discussions	$ XXX
Financial Perspective	Increase non-gov't funding	Amount of funding	Amount of funds	Identify possible grant opportunities	$ XXX
Funding	Maintain cost of living increases in gov't funding	Amount of Government funding	Government budget	Meet with stakeholders for lunch	$ XXX
	Increase materials budget	Materials budget	Materials budget		

Figure 7.1. Overview of the Balanced Scorecard Process. Adapted from Robert S. Kaplan and David P. Norton, "How Strategy Maps Frame an Organization's Objectives," *Financial Executive* (March/April 2004): 40–45.

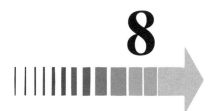

8

Step 5: Integrating the Scorecard

Not everything that can be counted counts. Not everything that counts can be counted.

—Albert Einstein[1]

STEP 5A—INTEGRATE THE LIBRARY'S SCORECARD

The real value of the scorecard will emerge as it is integrated into the life of the library. The scorecard will be a focal point of discussion within departmental and other group meetings in the library. It will also be a topic of conversation among the library's management team when they meet with the library funding decision makers. All of these activities will take some time to happen, as shown in Figure 8.1.

During the time that the library is developing its initial scorecard (the "design" phase shown in Figure 8.1), the scorecard team is mobilized, the library's strategy is articulated, performance measures and targets are selected, and project initiatives are identified. During the "implement" phase, the scorecard is communicated to the key library stakeholders and all library staff members. The scorecards are typically updated on a quarterly basis.

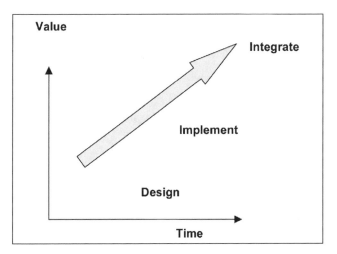

Figure 8.1. Scorecard Implementation

Subsequently the scorecard team will work with other departments and branches to cascade the scorecard so that it is embedded further within the organization. The challenge is to use the cascading scorecard to help library units improve so that the entire library will achieve its targets. Some organizations have noted that the scorecard can engender negative results when it is used as a tool in a "win-lose" game.

During the "integrate" phase, the library has the opportunity to more carefully analyze any gaps in performance, identify and resolve issues that arise, allocate resources in a more strategic manner, and communicate the library's accomplishments to its stakeholders in a more consistent way.

A strategy-focused organization embodies four key principles:

- **Align** strategic and operational planning and budgeting to optimize strategy execution

- **Adapt** quickly to change through continuous planning and forecasting

- **Assign** and reallocate resources dynamically through initiative management (The budget will need to be reviewed and adjustments made in order to support the initiatives.)

- **Reduce** the detail and effort in the planning process to achieve greater planning effectiveness and value

> *The more purposeful, effective data these days are outcomes and performance measures that show what good libraries do and how well they perform given their human and financial resources.*
>
> —Denise Troll Covey[2]

Developing and implementing a balanced scorecard requires a significant amount of change within the organization. The library might wish to embrace the eight steps for successful large-scale change suggested by John Kotter and Dan Cohen:

- Increase urgency—reduce the fear, complacency, and anger that prevent change from starting

- Build the guiding team—help the team behave with trust and emotional commitment to one another

- Get the vision right—create the right compelling vision to engender enthusiasm

- Communicate for buy-in—use words, deeds, and technology to unclog communication channels and overcome confusion and distrust

- Empower action—remove barriers that block those who have embraced the vision and strategies

- Create short-term wins—build momentum by making successes visible

- Don't let up—eliminate needless work and don't allow urgency to slacken

- Make change stick—ensure that people continue to act in new ways by using the power of emotion to enhance new group norms[3]

STEP 5B—CASCADE THE SCORECARD

After the library has updated its scorecard once or twice, it should ask branch libraries and selected departments to develop their own scorecards. This process is called cascading the scorecards (see Figure 8.2).

The lower level scorecards should utilize the same structure for the strategy map and some of the same performance measures. However, some performance measures will be unique for these lower level scorecards. The idea is to develop a lower level scorecard that supports the attainment of the library's broader targets and vision. However, the lower level scorecards must link back to the library balanced scorecard.

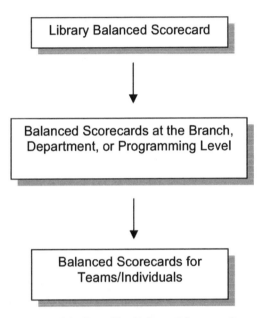

Figure 8.2. Cascading Balanced Scorecards

Developing departmental (functional) scorecards will eliminate the "competition" that may arise if branch library scorecards are used. Note that the branch libraries should all have the same balanced scorecard and use the same measures for each facility's scorecard. This provides a consistent focus, the same set of measures, and consistent presentation of results.

One of the major benefits of cascading the library's scorecard is that each of the lower level units within the library will have a better understanding of how its activities contribute to the library's ability to achieve its vision. For example, one of the library's broad measures might be the ability for each desktop computer to consistently access the required software applications. A balanced scorecard for the information technology group might have several unique measures that gauge the reliability of the various components—network, servers, desktops, and application software—that contribute to the overall reliability of the system.

Library managers should be encouraged to present and discuss the library's balanced scorecard and the department or facility balanced scorecard at all meetings. The library's scorecards must become a part of the library's culture. Thinking of the scorecard as a one-time project will doom the effort to develop and use a scorecard to failure.

One study found that in poorly performing organizations, some two-thirds of employees did not have a good understanding of overall organizational goals.[4]

> *The nonprofit must be information-based. It must be structured around information that flows up from the individuals doing the work to the people at the top—the ones who are, in the end, accountable—and around information flowing down. This flow of information is essential because a nonprofit organization has to be a learning organization.*
>
> —Peter F. Drucker[5]

STEP 5C—MANAGEMENT'S FOCUS

> *Without the right words, used in the right way, it is unlikely that the right actions will occur. Words do matter—they matter very much. Without words we have no way of expressing strategic concepts, structural forms, or designs for performance measurement systems. In the end, there is no separating action from rhetoric.*
>
> —Robert G. Eccles and Nitin Nohria[6]

The results of the scorecard should be candidly discussed during departmental and other meetings involving staff members. Managerial and departmental meetings should focus on implementing the library's strategies rather than simply trying to cope with the inevitable fires and problems that seem to arise faster than an Internet virus.

Discussions about implementation problems concerning one or more of the initiatives that the library has embarked upon are more specifically focused due to the use of the scorecard. Everyone has a chance to see the big picture and know how what he or she does contributes to the library achieving its ultimate vision.

It's very important to discuss each of the measures and the progress the library is making in achieving its targets. Discussing the measures, how the data are collected, and, most important, what the data mean is crucial to the success of developing and updating the library's balanced scorecard. Remember that the scorecard is a tool for the management of the library to better serve its community and communicate the activities and accomplishments of the library to the various stakeholders.

It is particularly important for the library director to do the following:

- Talk to and highlight progress with stakeholders and the library management team. Consistently use every opportunity to encourage and highlight progress in your library.

- Acknowledge the contribution of library staff members. A library scorecard means change. Help staff when they have doubts, encourage them when they try, coach them when they fail, and celebrate when they achieve a goal.

- Support learning from mistakes, rethinking, and adjustments. As you gain experience using a scorecard, you will make changes in the choice of performance measures, targets, and initiatives.

- Reinforce the notion that the scorecard is here to stay, not just another project or initiative.

During the second year of using the library's scorecard, the management team should have a realistic discussion about the measures and targets included in the scorecard. Among the questions that should be addressed are the following:

- Are the strategies articulated by the library working?

- Does the library need new performance measures that will better reflect the actual performance of the library?

- Are there any measurement problems?

- Could data for a particular measure be gathered in a more cost-effective and less labor-intensive manner?

- Were the original short-term and long-term targets realistic?

- Did any special circumstances arise during the year that affected the library and its scorecard?

- Were all of the initiatives completed in a timely manner?

- Did each initiative positively affect the library?

- What will fix a specific problem (staffing, funding, process improvement, other resources)?

- Should the library discontinue one or more existing services?

- Has planning been linked to the budgeting process?

Every library's scorecard will evolve and change as the library continues to adjust its priorities and services to better meet the needs of its customers. The library should not feel any pressure to get it "right" but rather acknowledge that the scorecard provides an intelligible framework for presenting information about the performance and value of the library. It is impossible to obtain perfect data, and more often than not, it is also unrealistic to expect to obtain near-perfect data. Focus on getting good enough data that will suffice for the purpose. After all, the whole purpose of evaluation and assessment of a library's services is to *improve* the library's services, collections, electronic resources, processes, and overall performance for its customers.

Libraries are apt to use a short-term solution to solve long-term problems. Using the balanced scorecard will assist the library in determining priorities of service and the market segments that will be principally served.

Integrating the scorecard into the library's culture will require change. "Business as usual" just won't work. Meetings must be organized around your strategies, your initiatives, and your perspectives. Make sure your meetings have a strategic focus rather than concentrating on operational problems.

> Organizations that have successfully integrated the balanced scorecard into their culture use it to drive the agendas of almost all meetings. The status of the various initiatives can be tracked and progress in meeting the targets can be assessed.

Developing and using a balanced scorecard is not

- quick and easy,
- a one-time effort,
- solely internally focused, or
- a new management technique *du jour*.

One of the keys to success in using a scorecard is going beyond the collection of performance measures to dig into the data, sometimes called analysis, so that the library management team can begin to understand the reality that the data represent. After all, *the purpose of analysis is insight.*

> **Tip!** Gathering, analyzing, and thinking about the performance measures is important, especially since these data will be collected over time. A useful resource to assist you in this process is Donald J. Wheeler's *Understanding Variation: The Key to Managing Chaos* (Knoxville, TN: SPC Press, 2000).

Recognition

The staff of the library need to be recognized when they do a good job. Aside from the obvious fairness of such a practice, recognition and incentives will improve performance. Several issues should be addressed when implementing a recognition program:

- **Recognition should be widely based.** Recognition should be fair and open to all who contributed to the improvement performance, as evidenced by improvements in the various performance measures selected for the scorecard.

- **Target a few early wins.** If there are some early victories, it is easier to build and maintain momentum. Celebrate success, celebrate failure!

- **Know what to reward.** It is advisable to have a wide range of rewards, from those for extraordinary achievement to those for ordinary accomplishments. Ask staff what should be rewarded and whom they think should be recognized.

- **Reward the producers.** If everyone is treated the same in terms of recognition and rewards, in the long run performance will never become outstanding.

- **Implement the program properly.** Recognition programs often fail due to poor implementation. The library's management team must demonstrate their commitment to the program. Any program requires visibility and ongoing budgetary support.

- **Choose appropriate methods of recognition.** There are several types of recognition:

- **Interpersonal recognition.** Listen to staff through the use of surveys, face-to-face discussions, and group meetings. Acting on what they say and suggest does much for morale. Dropping by to give praise or a congratulatory e-mail is often all that is necessary.

- **Symbolic recognition.** A low-cost but effective option is use of certificates of appreciation or gift cards for movies or meals.

- **Financial rewards.** Modest financial rewards have been used to great effect in some libraries.

- **External recognition.** A number of awards are given for effective public management.

Implementation Challenges

Not surprisingly, development of a balanced scorecard can be problematic. Based on the literature, the issues that may arise include the following:

- **Time involved.** The entire process to develop the initial scorecard may range from eight to fifteen days, spread out over two to four months. The amount of time depends in part on how well the scorecard team works together and the level of their commitment to reading the suggested readings and thinking about making the scorecard work in the library.

- **The perfect measures.** Some organizations spend too much time searching for the "perfect set of measures." Recognize at the outset that a workable set of measures is a great place to start and that adjustments and changes will occur over time.

- **Encountering resistance.** Any change may alter patterns of communication, working relationships, and control, and thus the library must plan for and mitigate the impact of the inevitable resistance to change.

- **Data collection problems.** Some measures may require the library to create a survey instrument, create a new data collection form, revise an existing form, and so forth. In addition, as attention is drawn to a particular measure, inconsistencies in how the data are gathered at different library facilities may emerge that will require attention and resolution.

- **Lack of meaningful staff involvement.** The scorecard team may not include a wide range of people in the process, so the resulting scorecard will be suspect or focused on the wrong measures. Share drafts of the library's strategy map, choice of performance measures, targets, initiatives, and the balanced scorecard periodically with staff members and stakeholders and ask for feedback.

- **Too many measures.** Information overload is likely to result if more than three to five measures per perspective are included. It is better to have fewer measures than too many.

- **Measures that do not focus on strategy.** The selected measures must be aligned with strategy; otherwise there is no way to assess the value of the strategy.

- **Automating the scorecard.** Although software is available to assist the library in creating its scorecard and analyzing the data, the library should resist the urge to automate. It is better to manually collect and update the scorecard so that its components are clearly understood. Data for the scorecard should be stored in a spreadsheet to make updating the scorecard easier in the future.

> *Remember! The library balanced scorecard is about management and change first; the use of performance measures is second.*

TIPS FOR SUCCESS

Clearly introducing a library balanced scorecard requires a considerable investment in staff time and other resources. The scorecard should be implemented in stages over time. If this is done correctly, it will have positive impact on the library's ability to deliver relevant and valuable services to its customers. It should not be surprising that some staff members will be resistant to change.

The library will have to manage the changes required. Some of the major issues that will have to be addressed are shown in Table 8.1.

Table 8.1. Keys and Processes for Making Change Happen[7]

Key Success Factors for Change	Questions for Accomplishing Change
Leading change (who is responsible)	Will the library director . . . • Own and champion the scorecard? • Demonstrate public commitment to making the scorecard happen? • Garner resources to sustain it? • Invest personal time and attention to seeing it to completion? • Communicate the concept of the scorecard to the library's stakeholders?
Creating a shared need (why do it)	Do staff members . . . • See the reasons for adopting a scorecard? • Understand why the scorecard is important? • See how it will help the library improve?
Shaping a vision (what the library will look like in the future)	Do staff members . . . • Recognize what changes in behavior they will need to make? • Become interested in and motivated to make improvements in the library? • Understand how changes will benefit the library's customers?

Key Success Factors for Change	Questions for Accomplishing Change
Mobilizing commitment (who else needs to be involved)	Does the management team . . . • Recognize who needs to be committed to the changes for them to happen? • Know how to build a coalition for support of the scorecard? • Have the ability to enlist the support of key individuals within the library? • Communicate frequently the library's vision and the role of the scorecard?
Building enabling systems	Does the management team . . . • Understand how to sustain and track the changes that will result from the projects and initiatives undertaken as a part of the balanced scorecard? • Have the flexibility in the budget to sustain change? • Have a communication plan for library staff? • Acknowledge the importance of performance measures?
Monitoring and demonstrating progress	Does the management team . . . • Have the skills to collect and analyze the data for the measures? • Publish quarterly updates to the library balanced scorecard for all staff and interested stakeholders? • Discuss the implications of the scorecard during management meetings on a regular basis?
Making it last (how will the scorecard be sustained)	Does the management team . . . • Have the commitment to keep attention focused on the scorecard? • Recognize that the scorecard will require adjustments over time? • Tie projects and initiatives to the scorecard? • Believe the scorecard helps them do a better job of communicating the value of the library to their stakeholders? • Post the scorecard?

Adapted from Brian E. Becker, Mark A. Huselid, and Dave Ulrich, *The HR Scorecard: Linking People, Strategy, and Performance* (Boston: Harvard Business School Press, 2001), 186.

NOTES

1. Sign hanging in Einstein's office at Princeton.

2. Denise Troll Covey, "Using Data to Persuade: State Your Case and Prove It," *Library Administration & Management* 19 no. 2 (Spring 2005): 82–89.

3. John P. Kotter and Dan S. Cohen, *The Heart of Change: Real-Life Stories of How People Change Their Organizations* (Boston: Harvard Business School Press, 2002).

4. William Fonvielle and Lawrence P. Carr, "Gaining Strategic Alignment: Making Scorecards Work," *Management Accounting Quarterly* 3, no. 1 (Autumn 2001): 4–15.

5. Peter F. Drucker, *Managing the Non-Profit Organization* (New York: HarperBusiness, 1990), 182.

6. Robert G. Eccles and Nitin Nohria, *Beyond the Hype: Rediscovering the Essence of Management* (Boston: Harvard Business School Press, 1992), 76.

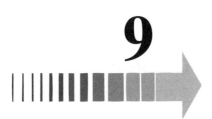

Step 6: Communicating Your Scorecard

SELECT A FORMAT FOR THE LIBRARY'S BALANCED SCORECARD

The scorecard concept is particularly useful in communicating to the library's stakeholders information about the library so that they can assess

- the extent to which the library has achieved predetermined targets, goals, and objectives;
- the trend in performance over time;
- the performance of the library relative to the performance of similar comparable libraries; and
- the performance relative to predetermined benchmarks.

After the library balanced scorecard has been developed and the measures, targets, and initiatives have been finalized, the library has a very important decision to make about how the scorecard is to be communicated to its stakeholders, be they the library's funding decision makers, campus administrators, staff members, library board members, library customers, or other interested parties.

Typically an organization will present its balanced scorecard either as a part of its annual report or as a separate document (usually a four- to eight-page brochure with colorful graphics). How the scorecard is presented is very important because it will have a major impact on the stakeholders' perception of the value of the scorecard and indirectly on the value of the library itself. The library needs to assess the culture within the library as well as how the funding decision makers would prefer to receive information about the library and its budget requirements before deciding which approach will be most effective. Among the options are

- a "dashboard,"
- the strategy map,
- a "spider web" diagram,
- the scorecard model of perspectives, and
- a combination of approaches.

Regardless of the approach selected, the library should prepare some explanatory text that describes the concept of the library balanced scorecard, explains the rationale for why the perspectives were selected, and describes the measures and their associated targets. In some cases, the library may also want to identify the initiatives it has undertaken to reach its targets.

The "Dashboard" Approach

Similar to the instrument panel found in an automobile or airplane, the library balanced scorecard dashboard provides a "quick glance" at how the library is doing (see Figure 9.1). Each instrument is calibrated to indicate the short-term and long-term goals. The current value of the performance measure is shown as the arrow. The results are often color coded, similar to a traffic signal, to more quickly convey the status of each instrument or performance measure. For example, measures that exceed the short-term or long-term targets are shown as green. Measures that come close to the short-term target are colored yellow. Measures that fall short are colored red.

For each dashboard instrument representing a particular perspective, an additional dashboard is shown that presents the current status of all the measures for that particular perspective (measures for the information resources perspective are shown in Figure 9.1).

The Strategy Map Approach

Some organizations use the strategy map they have developed together with the measures associated with each perspective (see Figure 9.2, page 94). Each measure is color coded (red, yellow, or green) to indicate the current status in terms of achieving the target. Green indicates that the target has been achieved or exceeded; yellow that the value of the measure is close to reaching the target; and red that the value of the measure is not close to reaching the target. Note that neither the value for all measures nor their associated targets are presented, although the information is available for those interested in the additional details.

The Spider Web Diagram Approach

The third approach uses a spider web diagram, sometimes called a radar diagram (see Figure 9.3, page 95). This approach has been used by a number of organizations to present a fair amount of information in a format that identifies the current value of each measure along with its associated target. Note that a line from the center is needed for each performance measure. Short-term and long-term targets can also be included, if desired. Targets should be equidistant from the center.

The Scorecard Approach

This approach, illustrated in Figure 9.4 (page 96), clearly identifies the perspectives along with the associated measures, targets, and initiatives that the library is undertaking to achieve its vision. Some organizations replace the descriptive approach for the targets and present the actual data in the form of line graphs or bar charts.

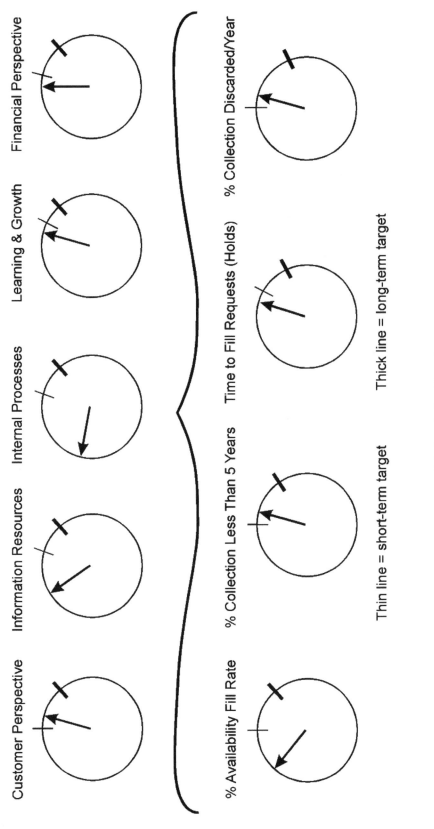

Figure 9.1. Sample Dashboard

93

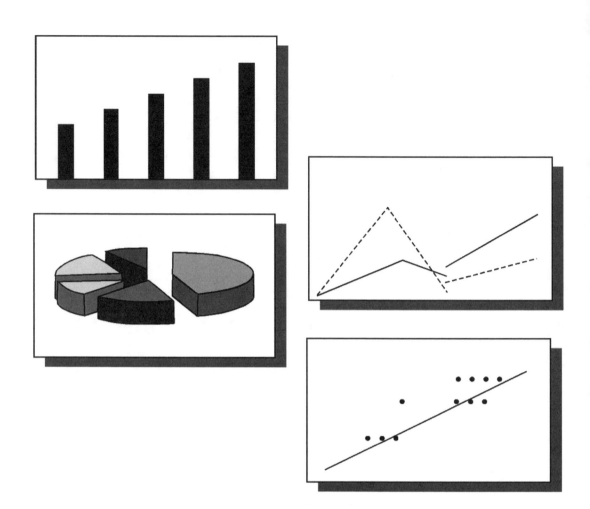

Figure 9.2. Various Ways to Present Data

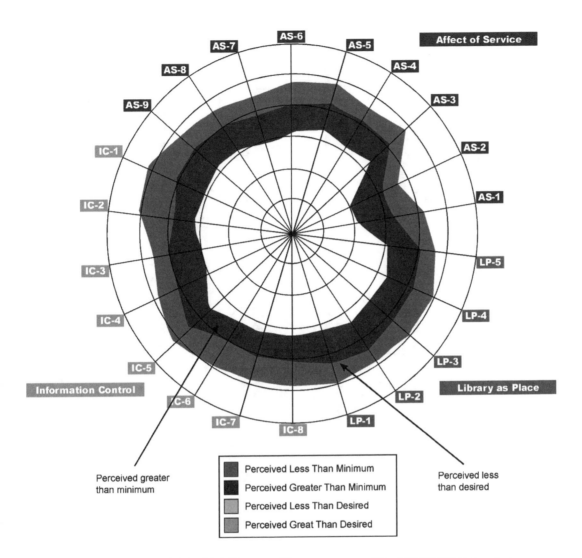

Figure 9.3. Sample Spider Web Diagram. Diagram courtesy of the ARL LibQUAL+ project

Our Vision

What Does It Mean to Our:		Measures	Targets	Initiatives
Customers	**Service & Value** To be frequently used and valued by the community	Cost/Benefit Analysis Customer Satisfaction % Population Who Use the Library in Last Year	Exceed 4:1 cost/benefit ration More than 96% Satisfied More than 55% of Population	Use focus groups to better identify customer needs Merchandize frequently used materials
Information Resources	**Relevant & Current** Provide access to a collection of materials and electronic databases that our customers find of value	% Collection Added in Last 5 Years Availability Rate - %	45% of Collection Added in Last 5 Years 80% Availability Rate	Train pages to read shelves Weed collection every 2 years
Internal Processes	**Customer Focused** To excel in anticipating and responding to customers needs	Time to reshelve materials Time to catalog & process materials Cost of staff/circulation	Reshelve within 4 hours Catalog & processing time of 7 work days Be in the lowest 25% quartile among peer libraries	Restructure flow of materials Explore outsourcing Use more self-checkout machines
Organizational Readiness	**Right People, Attidude & Tools** To attract and retain committed staff members that utilize the required tools to deliver quality services	Staff competencies assessment Staff morale Network reliability	90% of staff have basic skills Morale rating in excess of 80% Network reliability in excess of 99.999% uptime	Provide training on a more regular basis Provide immediate staff recognition rewards Identify ISP options
Stakeholders	**Demonstrate Value** Demonstrate that the library's services are valued by the community	Library budget per capita % grants applied & received Dollar value of contributions	Funding = COL increases Win 35% of grants Contributions exceed $150,000	Hire full-time grant writer Expanded space for Friends book sale in library

Figure 9.4. The Scorecard Approach

The Combination Approach

The final approach combines the strategy map approach with the scorecard approach so that the specific strategies being utilized by the library are identified along with an indication of the current value of each measure and its associated targets.

PREPARING THE BROCHURE

After the particular approach has been selected, the data for each of the measures should be gathered and the library's balanced scorecard brochure should be prepared. The text should include an introduction of the concept of the scorecard along with an explanation of the particular model that has been developed by the library, together with a description of the rationale behind the scorecard. The library should utilize the services of a graphic designer in order to prepare a scorecard brochure that will be attractive and encourage the reader to carefully review the material.

Remember that a picture is worth a thousand words. Data can be displayed in a wide variety of way, including graphic presentations such as histograms (bar charts), pie charts, line charts, and scatter diagrams.

The presentation of data can be summarized as part of the scorecard, and more detailed data along with a discussion of the implications can be presented at the end of the scorecard. For example, while the average may be provided for a particular measure, additional value will result if the range and distribution are provided to demonstrate the complexity of the issue. Often the raw performance measure will have little meaning to most people. Adding value to performance measures takes the form of context, visualization, trends, and comparisons to the results of other libraries.

The intent of the scorecard is to accomplish two things: 1) communicate to the library staff the progress the library is making in achieving its vision and 2) communicate the value of the public library to its stakeholders and the local community. Making the best possible impression in terms of an attractive presentation is a basic requirement.

A further discussion should be presented to identify the particular measures, the targets, and the initiatives the library has undertaken. This "draft" version of the library's scorecard should then be shared with the library's stakeholders for review. The stakeholders are likely to need one or two weeks to review and digest the "draft" library balanced scorecard in order to offer constructive comments.

The library director or the library scorecard team leader should schedule a meeting to receive feedback from the various stakeholders. The library staff should carefully listen to the comments of the stakeholders so that the final product can be improved upon to become something the stakeholders will understand and find to be of value.

Developing the library's balanced scorecard can be an effective tool for helping focus staff members on the most important services and activities. The scorecard will also be helpful in communicating the library's value to its various stakeholders. However, the scorecard must be complemented with the use of success stories about the library and its impact on its community. Storytelling is one of the most effective ways to persuade and convince![1]

A number of pitfalls should be avoided when preparing your scorecard:

- Do not list numbers using tables; rather, use some form of graphic or visual presentation to improve understanding.

- Do not choose visuals or graphic techniques unrelated to the data being presented.

- Do not present information that will be difficult for stakeholders to understand.

- Avoid too many colors and color schemes.

- Do not use library acronyms or jargon.

TIPS FOR TELLING YOUR LIBRARY'S STORY

Regardless of the format that your library selects to communicate the balanced scorecard, the library must provide some context to both introduce the scorecard concept and explain some of the important points that a nonlibrarian would not understand when looking at some of the measures. The presentation must also o be clear and understandable to people who have not participated in the process.

Among the points to remember are the following:

- **Know your audience.** Remember that you are communicating to the library's most important stakeholders who, in most cases, control the financial purse strings.

- **Leave the jargon at home.** Be straightforward, use clear English, and avoid technical and library terminology.

- **Be honest.** Your credibility is improved when you report the library's weaknesses as well as its accomplishments.

Everything you need for your better future and success has already been written. And guess what? It's all available. All you have to do is go to the library.

—Jim Rohn[2]

COMMUNICATING THE SCORECARD

Most organizations update their balanced scorecards on a quarterly basis (recognizing that some measures may only be updated once or twice a year). The library's scorecard is then shared with the appropriate funding decision makers and other interested stakeholders.

A number of organizations post their scorecards on their Web sites. Others create large posters and post the updated scorecard where staff members will see it and be reminded of the targets the library is striving to achieve. At the end of the library's fiscal year, consider putting together a brochure that describes the balanced scorecard, the strategies that are being employed, the choice of measures, and the targets and initiatives, to be distributed to all staff members.

The most important benefit of the scorecard is its use in facilitating communication about strategy throughout the organization!

A very important, and obvious, group of individuals who will be interested in your library's scorecard are your staff, governing body, volunteers, and support groups. Some of the likely questions that these individuals will want answers to include:

- What is a balanced scorecard?

- Why is our library embracing the scorecard concept?

- Why do we need to change and improve?

- What is the library's strategy?
- What are the relationships among and between the different perspectives?
- Why were the various performance measures selected and included in the scorecard?
- Are the targets achievable?
- How does what I do affect the measures included in the library's balanced scorecard?
- How close is the library to reaching the various targets?
- What initiatives and projects is the library implementing that will assist in reaching its targets?

The library's management team should prepare a comprehensive communications plan to introduce the library balanced scorecard because it will likely involve a fair amount of change in the library. The library might want to consider the following means of communication:

- **Town-hall style meetings** to explain to all staff members the concept of the scorecard and the rationale behind the library's balanced scorecard. This would be followed by a question-and-answer session.
- **Posters, brochures, newsletters, and a scorecard Web page.**
- **Formal and intensive training for all staff members.**

The library's scorecard should be shared with people inside and outside the library, as shown in Figure 9.5.

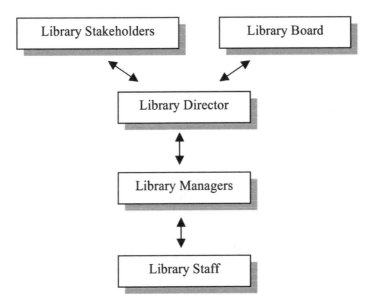

Figure 9.5. Communicating the Scorecard

Among the activities that should be considered part of introducing and updating the scorecard are to

- plan and schedule rollout meetings and presentations;
- include brief articles in the library's internal and external newsletters;
- distribute printed versions of the library's balanced scorecard;

- prepare supporting materials (e.g., PowerPoint™ slides, handouts and so forth);
- develop a set of FAQs (frequently asked questions) and post them on the library's Web site;
- provide classes to demystify the subject of measurement and the scorecard;
- provide copies of the quarterly updates to the library's scorecard (in print and on the library's Web site);
- discuss the latest scorecard in departmental meetings;
- provide informal sessions (e.g., brown-bag lunches) to discuss the library's scorecard;
- emphasize the benefits of adopting and using the scorecard;
- encourage staff to submit questions and issues about the library's scorecard; and
- consistently communicate the library's scorecard to stakeholders, staff, and customers (to be done by the entire management team, not just the library director).

Once the library starts updating the scorecard on a regular basis, hold regular "town hall" meetings led by the library's scorecard team. During these meetings candidly discuss such questions as:

- What is the library's actual performance?
- How does our actual performance compare with the established targets?
- What are some of the reasons the targets are not being met?
- What is the plan for corrective action?
- Are there any suggestions from staff for improvements?
- Have any actions been taken so far?
- Will the planned action have the desired impact on the results of the measures?

Remember! The library balanced scorecard is a means to an end, not an all-encompassing purpose for action. You will need to sell the concept of a library balanced scorecard to your library's various stakeholders. Never assume you will have support!

The publisher, Libraries Unlimited, will provide a pdf file containing samples of strategy maps and library scorecards that have been developed by a number of different types of libraries. Check it out at http://lu.com/scorecards!

NOTES

1. Stephen Denning, *The Springboard: How Storytelling Ignites Action in Knowledge-Era Organizations* (New York: Butterworth-Heinemann, 2001).

2. Jim Rohn, *The Treasury of Quotes* (South Lake, TX: Jim Rohn International, 2001).

Glossary

Activities. Programs or services provided to the library's customer.

Balanced scorecard. A tool providing a comprehensive framework that translates an organization's vision and strategy into a coherent set of performance measures.

Baseline data. Initial collection of data to establish a basis for comparison, evaluation, and target setting.

Benchmark. A standard or point of reference used in measuring and judging quality or value.

Benchmarking. The process of continuously comparing and measuring an organization against recognized leaders anywhere in the world to gain information that will help the organization take action to improve its performance. Comparing metrics between libraries or peer organizations.

Best-in-class. Outstanding performance within an industry or sector; synonyms include "best practice" and "best-of-breed."

Best practice. Superior performance in an activity, regardless of industry, leadership, management, or operational approaches; methods that lead to exceptional performance. A relative term that indicates innovative or interesting business practices that have been identified during a particular benchmarking study as contributing to improved organizational performance.

Cause and effect. The relationship among strategic themes and their impact on one another.

Continuous improvement. Ongoing, incremental steps taken to enhance service delivery by improving efficiency and effectiveness.

Critical success factors. Those things that must be done right if the vision is to be achieved; characteristics, conditions, or variables that have a direct influence on a customer's satisfaction with a specific process.

Customer. The person or group that establishes the requirements of a process and receives or uses the outputs of that process, or the person or entity directly served by the organization. Synonyms in a public library include "patron," "borrower," "guest," and "user."

Evaluation. Measurement or verification of inputs, processes, outputs, and outcomes using performance indicators or measures.

Goal. Broad statements describing desired outcomes, but more specific than an agency's mission; they support the mission and identify specific themes or opportunities for a library to address to achieve its mission.

Initiatives. The projects and programs that will achieve the library's performance goals.

Inputs. Resources (budget, staff, facilities, and so forth) used to plan and provide a service or program.

Key performance indicator. A measurable factor of extreme importance to the organization in achieving its strategic goals and objectives.

Lagging indicator. Performance measures that represent the consequences of actions previously taken.

Leading indicator. Performance measures that are considered the "drivers" of organizational performance.

LibQUAL+. A suite of services, provided by the Association of Research Libraries, that libraries use to solicit, track, understand, and act on users' opinions of service quality.

Measure. A quantifiable unit that provides information about the volume, financial performance, service quality, and results of a service.

Metrics. Measures or categories of information that define the overall performance of an organization, such as, productivity, satisfaction, etc.

Mission. A short, comprehensive description of why an organization exists. It succinctly identifies what an organization does (or should do), and for whom.

Outcome. Impacts or benefits to the library's customers, usually a change or gain in skills, knowledge, behavior, attitude, or condition/status.

Outputs. Units of service (counts of activities) resulting from the inputs and processes (activities) of the library.

Performance management. The use of performance measurement information to help set performance goals, allocate and prioritize resources, inform managers to either confirm or change current strategies or program directions to meet those goals, and report on the success of meeting those goals.

Performance measurement. A process of assessing progress toward achieving predetermined goals, including information on the efficiency with which resources are transformed into goods and services (outputs); the quality of those outputs, that is, how well they are delivered to customers and the extent to which customers are satisfied (service quality); and the qualitative results of a service compared to its intended purpose (outcome).

Perspectives. Different views of an organization.

Process owner. The individual who possesses control over a particular process or practice.

Process redesign. The re-engineering of processes, organizational structures, management systems, and values of an organization to achieve breakthroughs in performance.

Root cause. The fundamental reason for a particular observation; the result of asking "why" at least five times to determine the basic cause in a chain of causal relationships.

Stakeholder. The universe of people with an interest in the library and its services.

Strategic direction. The organization's goals, objectives, and strategies by which it plans to achieve its vision, mission, and values.

Strategic goal. A long-range target that guides an organization's efforts in moving toward a desired future state.

Strategic objective. A time-based measurable accomplishment required to realize the successful completion of a strategic goal.

Strategic planning. A continuous and systematic process whereby an organization makes decisions about its future, develops the necessary procedures and operations to achieve that future, and determines how success is to be measured.

Strategy. The means by which an organization intends to create sustained value for its stakeholders; how the organization intends to accomplish its vision and goals; its approach or "game plan."

Strategy map. A visual framework to illustrate the cause-and-effect relationships that support the organization's value-creating processes.

SWOT (strengths, weaknesses, opportunities, and threats) analysis. An organization's self-assessment of its strengths and weaknesses (internal factors) as well as opportunities and threats (external factors).

Target. A mark to shoot for; a short-term goal to be achieved. In some cases, short-term or interim targets are established as well as long-term targets.

Total quality management. A customer-focused management philosophy and strategy that seeks continuous improvement in organizational processes by applying analytical tools and teamwork.

Vision. A description of what and where an organization wants to be in the future.

World class. Leading performance in a process, independent of industry or geographic location.

Appendix: Selected Resources

BALANCED SCORECARDS

Birch, Charles. *Future Success: A Balanced Scorecard Approach to Measuring and Improving Success in Your Organization.* New York: Prentice Hall, 2000.

Bourne, Mike, and Pippa Bourne. *Balanced Scorecard in a Week.* London: Hodder & Stoughton, 2002.

Brown, Mark Graham. *Winning Score: How to Design and Implement Organizational Scorecards.* Portland, OR: Productivity, 2001.

Butler, Alan, Steve R. Letza, and Bill Neale. "Linking the Balanced Scorecard to Strategy." *Long Range Planning* 30, no. 2 (1997): 242–53.

Ceynowa, Klaus. "Managing Academic Information Provision with the Balanced Scorecard: A Project of the German Research Association." *Performance Measurement & Metrics* 1, no. 3 (December 2000): 157–64.

Chan, Yee-Ching Lilian. "Performance Measurement and Adoption of Balanced Scorecards: A Survey of Municipal Governments in the USA and Canada." *International Journal of Public Sector Management* 17, no. 3 (2004): 204–21.

Chow, Chee W., Kamal M. Haddad, and James E. Williamson. "Applying the Balanced Scorecard to Small Companies." *Management Accounting* (1997): 21–27.

Eccles, Robert G. "The Performance Measurement Manifesto." *Harvard Business Review* (January–February 1991): 131–37.

Epstein, Marc, and Jean-Francois Manzoni. "Implementing Corporate Strategy: From Tableaux de Bord to Balanced Scorecards." *European Management Journal* 16, no. 2 (April 1998): 190–203.

Kaplan, Robert S. "Strategic Performance Measurement and Management in Nonprofit Organizations." *Nonprofit Management & Leadership* 11, no. 3 (Spring 2001): 353–70.

Kaplan, Robert S., and David P. Norton. "The Balanced Scorecard—Measures That Drive Performance." *Harvard Business Review* 69, no. 1 (January/February 1992): 71–79.

———. *The Balanced Scorecard: Translating Strategy Into Action.* Boston: Harvard Business School Press, 1996.

———. "Devising a Balanced Scorecard Matched to Business Strategy." *Harvard Business Review* 72, no. 5 (September/October 1994): 15+.

———. "Having Trouble with Your Strategy? Then Map It." *Harvard Business Review* 78, no. 5 (September/October 2000): 167–76.

———. "How Strategy Maps Frame an Organization's Objectives." *Financial Executive* (March/April 2004): 40–45.

———. "Linking the Balanced Scorecard to Strategy." *California Management Review* 39, no. 1 (1996): 53+.

————. "Measuring the Strategic Readiness of Intangible Assets." *Harvard Business Review* 82 (February 2004): 52–63.

————. "Putting the Balanced Scorecard to Work." *Harvard Business Review* 71, no. 5 (September/October 1993): 134–47.

————. *The Strategy-Focused Organization*. Boston: Harvard Business School Press, 2001.

————. *Strategy Maps: Converting Intangible Assets Into Tangible Outcomes*. Boston: Harvard Business School Press, 2004.

————. "Using the Balanced Scorecard as a Strategic Management System." *Harvard Business Review* 74, no. 1 (1996): 75–85.

Lingle, John H., and William A. Schiemann. "From Balanced Scorecard to Strategy Gauges: Is Measurement Worth It?" *Management Review* 85, no. 3 (March 1996): 55–61.

Matthews, Joseph R. "The Library Balanced Scorecard: Is It in Your Future?" *Public Libraries* 45, no. 6 (November/December 2006): 64–71.

Meyer, Christopher. "How the Right Measures Help Teams Excel." *Harvard Business Review* 70, no. 3 (May/June 1994): 95–103.

Niven, Paul R. *Balanced Scorecard Step-by-Step: Maximizing Performance and Maintaining Results*. New York: Wiley, 2003.

Pathak, Susanna. "The People Side of Planning and Implementing a Large Scale Balanced Scorecard Initiative." In *Proceedings of the Library Assessment Conference. Building Effective, Sustainable, Practical Assessment, September 25–27, 2006, Charlottesville, Virginia,* 303–18. Washington, DC: Association of Research Libraries, 2007.

Pienaar, Heila, and Cecilia Penzhorn. "Using the Balanced Scorecard to Facilitate Strategic Management at an Academic Information Service." *Libri* 50 (2000): 202–9.

Scholey, Cam. "Strategy Maps: A Step-by-Step Guide to Measuring, Managing and Communicating the Plan." *Journal of Business Strategy* 26, no. 3 (2005): 12–19.

The Society of Management Accountants of Canada. *Applying the Balanced Scorecard*. Mississauga, ON: The Society of Management Accountants of Canada, 1999.

DATA COLLECTION METHODOLOGIES

Schmidt, Faye, and Teresa Strickland. *Client Satisfaction Surveying: A Manager's Guide*. Ottawa, ON: Canada School of Public Service, 1998.

————. *Client Satisfaction Surveying: Common Measurement Tool*. Ottawa, ON: Canada School of Public Service, 1998.

PROCESS IMPROVEMENT

Culbertson, Amy, Archester Houston, Debbie Faast, Michael White, Monica Aguirre, and Carol Behr. *The Process Improvement Handbook*. Arlington, VA: Department of the Navy, 2001. Available at http://www.balancedscorecard.org/files/pin.pdf.

Handbook for Basic Process Improvement (PIN). Arlington, VA: Department of the Navy, 1996. Available at http://www.balancedscorecard.org/files/bpihndbk.pdf.

Houston, Archester. *Survey Handbook*. Arlington, VA: Department of the Navy, 1998. Available at http://www.balancedscorecard.org/files/surveyhb.pdf.

Houston, Archester, and Steven L. Dockstader. *Total Quality Leadership: A Primer*. Arlington, VA: Department of the Navy, 2000. Available at http://www. balancedscorecard.org/files/primer.pdf.

ONLINE SURVEY TOOLS

Searching for "online survey software" using an Internet search engine will result a number of products that offer a variety of templates for constructing your own survey, as well as standard surveys. Among the more popular options are the following:

SurveyMonkey. Available at http://www.surveymonkey.com.

WebSurveyor. Available at http://www.websurveyor.com.

Zoomerang. Available at http://www.zoomerange.com.

OUTCOME MEASURES

Bond, Sally L., Sally E. Boyd, and Kathleen A. Rapp, with Jacqueline B. Raphael and Beverly A. Sizemore. *Taking Stock: A Practical Guide to Evaluating Your Own Programs*. Chapel Hill, NC: Horizon Research, Inc., 1997. Available at http://horizon-research.ca/city_services/grants/toolkit/index_en.shtml.

Corporation for National Service. *Toolkit: A User's Guide to Evaluation for National Service Programs*. Available at http://www.projectstar.org/star/Library/toolkit.html.

Dresang, E. T., M. Gross, and Glen E. Holt. "Project CATE: Using Outcome Measures to Assess School-Age Children's Use of Technology in Urban Public Libraries: A Collaborative Research Process." *Library and Information Science Research* 25, no. 1 (2003): 19–42.

Durance, Joan C., and Karen E. Fisher. *How Libraries and Librarians Help: A Guide to Identifying User-Centered Outcomes*. Chicago: American Library Association, 2005.

Harvey, Jan, ed. *Evaluation Cookbook*. Edinburgh, Scotland: Institute for Computer Based Learning, 1998. Available at http://icbl.hw.ac.uk/ltdi/cookbook.

Institute of Museum and Library Services. *New Directives, New Directions: Documenting Outcomes in IMLS Grants to Libraries and Museums*. Washington, DC: Institute of Museum and Library Services, 2001. Available at http://www.imls.gov/grants/current/cmt_obebasics.htm.

Rockwell, Kay, and Claude Bennett. *Targeting Outcomes of Programs no. TOP). A Hierarchy for Targeting Outcomes and Evaluating Their Achievement*. Available at http://citnews. uni.edu/TOP/english/index.html.

Rudd, Peggy D. "Documenting the Difference: Demonstrating the Value of Libraries Through Outcome Measurement." In *Perspectives on Outcome Based Evaluation for Libraries and Museums*. Washington, DC: Institute of Museum and Library Services, 2000. Available at http://www.imls.gov/pubs/pdf/pubobe.pdf.

Steffan, Nicolle O., and Keith Curry Lance. "Who's Doing What: Outcome-Based Evaluation and Demographics in the Counting on Results Project." *Public Libraries* (September/October 2002): 271–79.

Steffan, Nicolle O., Keith Curry Lance, and Rochelle Logan. "Time to Tell the Whole Story: Outcome-Based Evaluation and the Counting on Results Project." *Public Libraries* (July/August 2002): 222–28.

Index

About the Author

JOSEPH R. MATTHEWS is an instructor at the San Jose State University School of Library and Information Science. He is also a consultant specializing in strategic planning, assessment and evaluation of library services, the use of performance measures, and the Library Balanced Scorecard. He lives in Carlsbad, California.